Praise for The TOP Sales Leader Playbook

"To win big deals sales leaders need a great team that can execute big plays. This playbook is packed with big plays from a brilliant team led by a great author/coach."

–STEVE HALL, AUSTRALIA'S LEADING C-LEVEL SALES AUTHORITY
MANAGING DIRECTOR OF EXECUTIVE SALES COACHING AUSTRALIA

"Companies may win one or two big contracts but in my experience, to truly have a big deal engine, a comprehensive approach is required. The TOP Sales Leader Playbook: How to Win 5X Deals Repeatedly is the answer. Lisa's latest book includes everything that the sales leadership team needs for complex contract success – time after time."

–ALICE HEIMAN, CHIEF REVENUE OFFICER, ALICE HEIMAN, LLC AND CO-FOUNDER, TRADESHOW MAKEOVER™

"As the VP of Sales my charter is clear – drive revenue for the company. I have had many years of experience with Lisa's approach to landing big deals and I can confidently say that her methodology and tools work. The TOP Sales Leader Playbook now adds everything the sales leadership team needs to know and do to create successful habits that will yield sustainable results."

–JASON PORTER, VP OF SALES & MARKETING, CAYUSE

"Concise and incisive, practical and tactical, plays that will get you all the way to the goal line. I highly recommend The TOP Sales Leader Playbook because it's packed with strategies you can use immediately, straight from sales leaders themselves!"

–DEB CALVERT, PRESIDENT OF PEOPLE FIRST PRODUCTIVITY SOLUTIONS AND AUTHOR OF *DISCOVER QUESTIONS® GET YOU CONNECTED* AND *STOP SELLING & START LEADING*

"Solid guidance for sales leaders with ambitions to consistently win big deals!"

–GEORGE BRONTÉN, FOUNDER & CEO, MEMBRAIN

"Truly large contract wins take months or years, and victories are only gained through careful planning and attention to strategy details. The TOP Sales Leader Playbook provides the sales leadership team with high impact Plays, how to construct them, deploy them and what to do if the account team gets off track. Each Play is paired with examples and a sideline coach's expert opinion on the Play. Incredibly powerful and a must read for all sales managers, directors and VPs."

—James Muir, author of *The Perfect Close* and VP of Sales, ShiftWizard

"As Lisa uncovered in her research, playbooks are not just for sales reps. Sales leaders that consistently drive big revenue gains year-over-year follow a proven approach to identifying, developing and landing high revenue contracts. The TOP Sales Leader Playbook: How to Win 5X Deals Repeatedly delivers those gains."

—Lisa Dennis, author of *Value Propositions that Sell* and Founder & President, Knowledgence

"Lisa has skillfully put together a practical guide for sales leaders paired with powerful input from sixteen sideline experts. Results-oriented sales leaders will love this playbook."

—Meridith Elliott Powell, Business Growth Expert & Keynote Speaker

"I was fortunate to read an advance copy of The TOP Sales Leader Playbook: How to Win 5X Deals Repeatedly. I appreciate the solid advice from someone who has been there/done that. Both strategic and practical, the information (from Lisa and guest experts) on how to win larger deals is crucial to sales leaders as well as sales reps. Most importantly, it can help put organizations on a solid leadership trajectory. Highly recommended."

—Christopher Ryan, CEO, Fusion Marketing Partners, Author of *B2B Revenue Playbook* and *Winning B2B Marketing*

"The TOP Sales Leader Playbook: How to Win 5X Deals Repeatedly has positive implications for sales leaders all over the globe. Sales VPs, managers and directors now have a template for big contract success that transcends country lines and helps all account based teams win more. Invaluable!"

—Zeenath Kuraisha, Founder & CEO Asia Pacific Sales & Marketing Academy

"Lisa has the knowledge, experience, and most importantly, the intellectual curiosity to teach the 'Hows' to create, and conduct major large-scale opportunities. Her hands-on experience as a first and second line leader made her one of the most distinguished sales leaders that I have ever seen lead. Her proven sales methodology will yield a visible, predictable, and repeatable outcome."

—JAY TYLER, CEO, JAY TYLER CONSULTING

"Sales organizations in all industries aspire to "close large deals" only to come in second or third in the selection process with little understanding of how or why. Lisa Magnuson's The TOP Sales Leader Playbook offers them a 'fast track' to what they need — an engine that drives predictable big contracts year in and year out."

—SUZANNE PALING, AUTHOR OF THE SALES LEADER'S PROBLEM SOLVER AND THE ACCIDENTAL SALES MANAGER. FOUNDER, SALES MANAGEMENT SERVICES

"Successful sales leaders know that account teams succeed with flawless execution of a well-defined strategic approach carried out over time. The TOP Sales Leader Playbook reveals how to construct that win plan."

—DANIEL ZAMUDIO, FOUNDER & CEO, PLAYBOOX

"One of my top priorities as a sales leader is to create a culture of winning big contracts. The TOP Sales Leader Playbook: How to Win 5X Deals Repeatedly just made my job a whole lot easier. It's filled with actionable Plays based on real world successes. What could be more valuable for busy sales leaders?"

—FRANK CAPOVILLA, SVP, GLOBAL SALES, OVUM

"The TOP Sales Leader Playbook is an original, best in class playbook, steeped in primary research and focused on the key plays in leadership, methodology, execution and culture that are most likely to produce big deal wins efficiently and repeatedly. Lisa Magnuson cuts through the chaos and clutter of a Sales VP's job to the essence of successful sales team performance."

—BARBARA WEAVER SMITH, FOUNDER & CEO, THE WHALE HUNTERS, INC. AND AUTHOR OF WHALE HUNTING AND WHALE HUNTING WITH GLOBAL ACCOUNTS

The TOP SALES LEADER PLAYBOOK

How to Win 5X Deals *Repeatedly*

LISA D. MAGNUSON

FOREWORD BY JILL KONRATH

Copyright © 2019 by Lisa D. Magnuson. All Rights Reserved.

This publication may not be reproduced, stored in a retrieval system, or transmitted in whole or in part, in any form or by any means, electronic, mechanical, photocopying, recording, or otherwise, except as permitted under Section 107 or 108 of the 1976 United States Copyright Act, without the prior written permission of the author. Requests for permission should be addressed to Lisa D. Magnuson, Top Line Sales, 3777 Rivers Edge Drive, Lake Oswego, OR 97034 or emailed to *Lisa@toplinesales.com*.

First Edition

ISBN 978-0-9982247-1-8

Book and Cover design by Wordzworth, United Kingdom

DEDICATION

*"I didn't have time to write a short letter,
so I wrote a long one instead."*

–MARK TWAIN

This playbook is dedicated to all my mastermind groups who know that every result is better (and easier) with a team of advisors behind you. Thank you for your thoughtful input and unwavering support year after year.

I also want to give a special shout out to the original members of my *Sales Executive Mastermind Group* (Sales VPs) who regularly inspire me with their dedication to the craft of sales leadership. Their unrelenting optimism and true grit translate into powerful motivators and achievements within their sales organizations. They climb that mountain every month carrying the heavy revenue banner, and it is enormously gratifying for me to see them succeed with the support of their peers to ease their burden a bit.

I would like to thank the generous contributions of the Sideline Coaches for each Play. I searched the world for exactly the right expert for each Play. Consequently, I ended up with sound opinions from Europe, Australia, Singapore and all corners of the U.S. (See Appendix 1)

The research for this Playbook included comprehensive interviews with 41 Sales VPs who graciously shared their biggest priorities and challenges and lent their perspective on what a Sales Leader Playbook could and should be. Their wisdom informed the end result you now hold in your hands. I am deeply grateful to each one of them. (See Appendix 2)

The numbers add up to something powerful!

This Playbook was inspired by over 35 years of living and learning in trenches as a seller, sales leader and sales consultant, struggling to win 5X deals.

This Playbook was informed by in-depth interviews with 41 Sales VP's.

This Playbook was enhanced by 16 Sideline Coaches providing their Expert Opinion for each Play.

All these numbers add up to the best of field proven practices and modern approaches for you, the reader, to win 5X deals *repeatedly* in your organization.

Enjoy Ringing the Bell with your numerous and ongoing victories!

TABLE OF CONTENTS

Foreword	xi
Introduction	xiii
The Research Base	xvii
Unique Terms	xxi
Intentionally Omitted	xxiii

PART 1 — SALES LEADERSHIP PLAYS — 1

Play 1	Inspire and Activate Account Teams	3
Play 2	Establish 5X Deal Sales Expectations	9
Play 3	Create a Blueprint for Cross-Functional Collaboration	15
Play 4	Mentor and Develop Account Teams	20
Play 5	Develop a 12-Month Cadence	37

PART 2 — SALES METHODOLOGY PLAYS — 41

Play 6	Commit to a Strategic Opportunity Model	43
	Advance One: Scoring Opportunities	52
	Advance Two: Gathering Insights	55
	Advance Three: Assigning Team and Resources	58
	Advance Four: Agreeing on Team Guidelines	60
	Advance Five: Mapping Relationships	62
	Advance Six: Constructing A Pre-Strategy SWOT Matrix	65
	Advance Seven: Charting Strategy	67

	Advance Eight: Designing Win Themes™	70
	Advance Nine: Engaging Executives	75
	Advance Ten: Finding Expansion Opportunities	80
	Advance Eleven: Tracking Progress	82
Play 7	Ramp Up Your Sales Process for Complex Opportunities	83
Play 8	Develop Competitive Blocking Strategies	92

PART 3 – SALES EXECUTION PLAYS — 101

Play 9	Designate and Enable Account Quarterbacks	103
Play 10	Install Pre-Call Planning Acumen	111
Play 11	Mobilize War Rooms	122
Play 12	Conduct Internal 5X Business Reviews (IBRs)	130

PART 4 – SALES CULTURE PLAYS — 137

Play 13	Build a 5X Deal Sales Culture	140
Play 14	Establish Executive Outreach Norms	146
Play 15	Celebrate 5X Wins across your Organization	155
Play 16	Debrief, Analyze and Define Repeatable Best Practices	161

Appendix 1	Sideline Coach: Expert Opinion Contributors	169
Appendix 2	Sales Leader Interviewees	173
Appendix 3	Custom Templates Available at *www.toplinesales.com*	176

About the Author — 179

FOREWORD

Landing bigger deals changes everything. You can stop worrying about meeting your numbers. Those mid-month panic attacks totally disappear. Sales turnover decreases. Even one big win energizes your sales force, inspiring other sellers to new heights. They love working for companies with a winning sales culture.

Plus, when you have a marquee list of reference clients, landing other big deals is so much easier. And you have the opportunity for so much more add-on business, which significantly reduces your cost of sale.

What could be better? That's why I wrote *Selling to Big Companies*. But I focused only on the early stages of the sales process. Once you get momentum going, you need new strategies–ones that help you win these 5X deals consistently, even against formidable competitors.

But it's a challenge to switch from a small deal to a big deal culture. Salespeople need to change their habits and their mindset. They need to learn new skills. As a sales leader you have to help them through this transition by providing guidance and structure. It's a time consuming, long-term effort, but one that yields transformational results.

If that's what you want to achieve, use The TOP Sales Leader Playbook. First off, Lisa Magnuson is an expert in winning big deals. I frequently refer her to my clients when they're involved in a game-changing sales opportunity, one that could take their company to a whole new level.

If you want to learn all her best practices–and how to apply them to your sales team– this is your "go to" guide. Each of the sixteen plays covers crucial information about the play's attributes, how to construct the play, concrete tools you can use, and how to deploy the play for winning results.

To keep you and your sales team from getting off track, Lisa identifies yellow and red flags and explains their associated remedies. Finally, you'll get a slew of practical examples, combined with expert advice from sales leaders like you who have implemented these 5X strategies successfully.

Imagine the impact of winning 5X deals. Not just one, but many. You'll blow your revenue targets out of the water and rally the entire organization around these big accounts. Even better, you'll keep your best people and attract more like them. These 5X wins are the "rising tide that lifts all boats."

Every sales leader who wants to win big contracts on a regular basis needs a copy of this playbook to highlight, flag, but mostly to internalize. You can make the shift to a big deal organization and in the process, your career will skyrocket as well.

Jill Konrath

Speaker | Sales Strategist | Bestselling Author of Selling to Big Companies, More Sales Less Time, SNAP Selling and Agile Selling

INTRODUCTION

Is this your story?

You're part of the sales leadership team. You're under tremendous pressure to hit your revenue number this year along with all your other competing priorities. However, your days are filled with people issues, small contract issues and nasty competitors, not to mention an inbox that's spilling over with problems that you have to resolve immediately. The fact of the matter is that you feel the heavy revenue and forecast burden on your back month after month, quarter after quarter and year after year.

Meet Mark, the VP of Sales for a fast-growing software company based in the Pacific Northwest. Mark's top priority is to instill the TOP Line Account™ methodology and discipline into his sales organization in order to close more big accounts. In his industry, a contract lost means a virtual lock-out for five years or more.

Mark has invested in advanced big deal training annually but struggles with his sellers' ability to put the concepts and tools into daily practice. His sales organization is not yet *in the habit* of doing everything necessary to win big contracts reliably.

Recently, Mark and his sales leadership team went through a 360° view of their approach to big contracts. They discussed and assessed sales leadership, big deal sales methodology, sales execution and sales culture. In the middle of the assessment, however, the entire team became overwhelmed. Their day-to-day problems consumed them. Where would they ever find the time to shore up important "big deal" elements such as mentoring the account quarterback or inspiring a strategic mindset throughout the organization?

Just as Mark's director and managers were ready to throw in the towel, he had an idea. Were there one or two things they could do now that would have a ripple effect on the many things that needed to be improved? The answer was YES!

If they could commit to doing war rooms (account strategy sessions) every month, then they could also accomplish other critical 5X deal elements such as setting expectations, coaching and pre-call planning. Mark could see the team's energy levels rise immediately. The more they discussed the carry-over impact of war rooms, the more they realized the long-term effects they might achieve. The sales leadership team left the assessment meeting with a renewed sense of optimism. Achieving both their short-term and long-term goals of landing larger contracts was well within reach.

* * *

Every sales organization needs an engine that generates massive contract wins – *repeatedly*. This playbook is for Sales VPs and their leadership teams who are committed to identify, develop and close 5X deals--five times your average contract size.

My research shows an alarming gap between the skill levels of sales leaders versus sellers when it comes to large, enterprise deal proficiency. The unfortunate result is that sales leaders are the *single point of failure* for complex contracts because they're distracted with the unending daily challenges and priorities. This playbook will bridge the gap. It's an invaluable single source reference guide for modern sales leaders who want to win big.

Sales leaders will directly benefit from the valuable insights of sixteen recognized thought leaders as sideline coach experts for each play.

The TOP Sales Leader Playbook: How to Win 5X Deals **Repeatedly** delivers the roadmap to grow revenues exponentially and drive leadership success.

I would like to suggest six ways to use this Sales Leader Playbook:

1. Read through all the content so you know what a valuable resource you now own.
2. Encourage your sales management team to use their copy as a reference guide, checking the appropriate topic as a just-in-time source of expert information, eliminating the need to re-create the wheel.

3 Use the book as a resource to on-board new sales managers and other sales leaders.

4 Share relevant sections with account teams (especially the account team quarterback) who drive truly big deals for your company.

5 Share relevant sections with your counterparts in other disciplines (such as Marketing, Professional Services, Inside Sales) who serve as extended members of the account team.

6 Share a copy with the executive team so they can be better equipped to back up your efforts.

Embark on the journey of creating a custom sales leader playbook unique to your organization. Top Line Sales can assist you with this effort in several ways, as you will learn along the way. I hope you will find yourself and your team within this Playbook and use it to cut through the everyday clutter to your core business of efficient 5X deals.

THE RESEARCH BASE

I derived topics for the Playbook from primary research consisting of more than forty hours of live, one-on-one interviews with forty-one Sales VPs from a variety of industries. I wanted to learn about their top priorities, challenges and proficiency levels with all aspects of their complicated jobs. These interviews shaped the book in a fundamental way.

Demographics. Of the 41, 63% had (at the time) the title VP of Sales, 29% Chief Revenue Officer or EVP/SVP, and 7% Director of Sales. Women make up 29% of the total. Sixty-eight percent went through formal sales leadership training at some point in their career, and 75% came up through the sales ranks, that is, sold as an individual contributor prior to assuming a sales leadership position. About half manage a direct sales force while half manage through a channel or a combination of direct and channel. All but five have sales managers or directors reporting to them.

The respondents represent all sizes of sales organizations: small (less than 20 sellers) = 46%; mid-size (21-60 sellers) = 34%; and large (over 60 sellers) = 19%.

They also represent a wide range of industries including advertising, aerospace, analytics, apparel, business communications, business services, finance/financial services, healthcare, insurance, IT services, legal software, manufacturing, marketing, outsourced sales, professional services, security, software, technology. See Appendix 2 for a list of Sales Leaders interviewed and visit *www.toplinesales.com* for the Infographic which highlights my findings.

Key Findings. I discovered the top 3 challenges to be the following:

1   Recruiting and retaining the best salespeople
2   Marketplace dynamics

3   Training and skill development for sellers

Additionally, Sales VPs face a list of second-tier challenges:

1   Commoditized product/marketing conditions
2   Lack of data to manage the business
3   Seller's ability to follow the sales process
4   Sales cycle is too long
5   Friction between internal groups/departments
6   Sales leader discipline to focus on what's most important
7   Keeping up with the pace of change

Respondents also reported challenges in achieving results, dealing with personnel, management issues, training decisions, and product/market areas. In total, approximately 51 unique challenges were listed by sales leaders, about twice that of priorities.

As I collated and analyzed the data from these interviews, I discovered four critical subdivisions of the Sales Leaders' interests:

- Sales Leadership
- Sales Methodology
- Sales Execution
- Sales Culture

These topics became the four major parts of my book, with all plays falling under one of these headings. You will see this graphic to illustrate each part:

In summary, forty-one Sales VP's told me what they wanted in a 5X deal playbook, including the following:

- Easy reference *Plays* so every sales leader can create a repeatable *big deal engine* for their teams
- Consistency within the sales leadership team to systematize a *large deal culture*
- A powerful reference source to help them prioritize *critical issues* versus day-to-day *fires*
- A template with common language to increase effective communication within the sales organization
- Practical how-tos and models that deliver time savings for busy sales leaders
- Methods to accelerate new sales leader on-boarding with the 5X deal methodology to identify, develop and close 5X contracts

That's what the book became – a Playbook derived from deep conversations with broadly representative Sales VPs and carefully designed to meet their expressed needs in four primary topic areas. Each of the book's four Parts begins with a brief discussion of research findings that gave rise to the Plays covering that topic.

So, while this is a Playbook, not a research study, I based it on thorough study of the needs and requests of the people for whom I wrote it.

UNIQUE TERMS

Several terms in this Playbook warrant a definition.

5X Deal – A contract, deal or opportunity that's valued at 5X your average deal size. If your average contract is worth 100K, then a 5X deal is worth 500K.

TOP Line Account™ – A TOP Line Account™ is your biggest and best prospect or current customer poised for expansion (or at risk for loss). TOP Line Account™ opportunities are generally worth at least 5x your average customer or prospect size. TOP Line Account™ opportunities are complex in nature and require a strategic approach and framework to obtain or retain, grow, and close. The TOP Line Account Way™ is a methodology or system designed to identify, develop and close large, complex opportunities.

The Strategy Brief – the Strategy Brief includes the high impact elements associated with 5X deals. The elements are also known as *Advances*. The Strategy Brief offers a comprehensive tool for each advance. The advances include Scoring Opportunities, Gathering Insights, Assigning the Team and Resources, Agreeing on Team Guidelines, Mapping Relationships, Constructing a Pre-Strategy SWOT, Charting the Strategy, Designing Win Themes™, Engaging Executives, Finding Expansion Opportunities and Tracking Progress.

Win Themes™ – Win Themes™ are carefully constructed themes that represent the three to four areas of overlap between your customer's or prospect's priorities and your strengths. This overlap is a sweet spot for alignment and receptivity. Win Themes™ are always unique in that they are 100% customized to an individual customer or prospect.

Developing Win Themes™ is critical before doing a presentation, demo or delivering a proposal. Compelling Win Themes™ are backed up with evidence that might include case studies, proof points, stories, data, and statistics.

The 48-Hour Rule™ – The 48-Hour Rule™, simply stated, stipulates that to maintain sales momentum you need to consider the correct follow-up or action within 48 hours after interest has been established. Why? Because after 48 hours, momentum is lost, mindshare has vanished, and new problems or opportunities have arisen. (As a caveat, the rule does not suggest that speed trumps quality.)

Sales Leadership Team – Throughout this Playbook, I will use the following terms: sales leader, Sales VP, sales manager, sales director, senior sales leader and channel manager; these all represent members of the sales leadership team.

SMART (S.M.A.R.T.) Goals – These are goals that meet the criteria of Specific, Measurable, Attainable, Relevant, and Timely, or Time-Bound.

Important note: Throughout this Playbook, I will use the following terms interchangeably: big deals, 5X deals, top opportunities, complex contracts, strategic accounts, whales, large deals, elephants and TOP Line Accounts™. TOP Line Account™ opportunities are generally worth at least 5X your average customer or prospect size.

INTENTIONALLY OMITTED

The author chose to intentionally omit the following topics from this Playbook:
- Sales compensation
- Sales structure
- Sales assessments (all types)
- Sales recruiting
- Sales training specifics
- Territory development
- Specific technology enablement tools, platforms or applications

PART ONE

Sales Leadership Plays

---

*"Management is doing things right;
leadership is doing the right things."*

–PETER F. DRUCKER

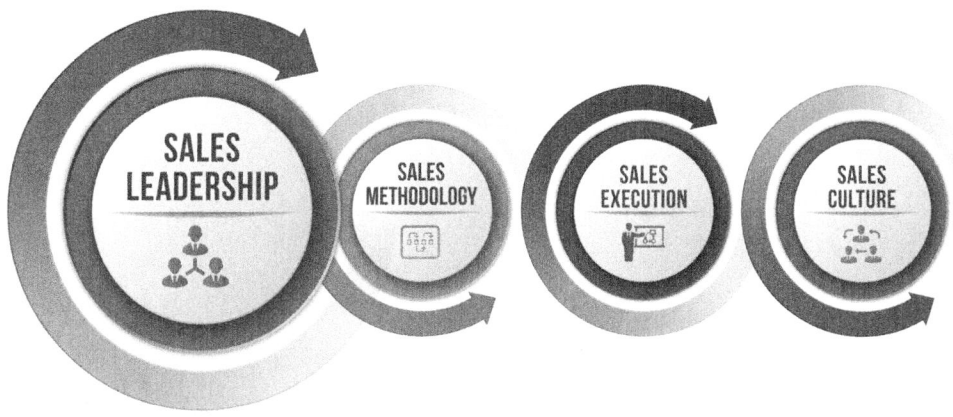

In this Part

Highly Effective Sales Leadership Teams inspire, establish, create, mentor and develop. Read on to learn how to:

- Inspire and activate account teams
- Establish 5X deal sales expectations
- Create a blueprint for cross functional collaboration
- Mentor and develop account teams
- Develop a 12 month cadence

Sales Leader Interview Findings

Top Line Sales, January 2019

I completed over 40 hours of live interviews with 41 Sales VP between February and October 2018. One of my key findings was this: an **Alarming Gap in Large Deal Proficiency.**

Sales leaders rated the majority (46%) of their sales managers as **experts** in large deal competency, while they rated the majority (53%) of their sellers as merely **proficient**: two levels down the scale from their managers! Pay attention to this–sales managers with large deal expertise seem unable to transfer this expertise to the sellers who report to them! The ramifications of this skill gap are substantial. Essentially, sales leaders can be the single point of failure if large deal development depends on their skills and expertise in training and coaching the sellers for whom they are responsible.

Part One: Sales Leadership Plays addresses this issue.

Take your team to the next level by creating your custom **Sales Leader Playbook**:

Downloadable templates make it easy for your sales leadership team to build your own unique approach to leadership, methodology, execution and culture for a 5X deal generating sales organization. No need to start from scratch. Customizable templates available at *www.toplinesales.com*.

PLAY #1

Inspire and Activate Account Teams

"Begin always expecting good things to happen."

–TOM HOPKINS

Play Attributes

It's appropriate that the first topic in this Sales Leader Playbook is about *inspiration*. This Play's purpose is to help sales leaders and managers understand their role in chartering, inspiring and activating account-based teams. Inspiring account teams means *leading with heart*.

Constructing the Play

- Account teams should be assembled and chartered by the sales leader.
- Sales leaders should mentor and pay special attention to account quarterbacks.
- Sales leaders must inspire and create passion within account teams so members will put in the hard work to win.
- Small victories lead to big successes, so it's imperative to celebrate all victories, big and small.

- Win celebrations go a long way to stimulate account teams to dig deep for the next huge contract sales opportunity.
- Intuitive sales leaders understand the driving motivation for each team member. They use personal encouragement to activate motivation. It's amazing how sellers can step up quickly with the proper input, encouragement and feedback.
- It's helpful for sales leaders to understand change management and how inspiration fits within the larger framework of helping account team members move through change if they are new to the work of winning 5X deals repeatedly.
- Astute sales leaders will monitor account team motivation regularly and address issues prior to red flag status.
- A *Big Deal* culture that encourages high achievement also tends to set a high benchmark for less than acceptable performance.

Deploying the Play

1. Sales leaders should set a cadence for opportunities to inspire teams. The general feeling throughout the organization should be that of a winning team. Perceptive sales leaders praise early and often.
2. Put big deal recognition on the calendar and make it clear, tied to big deal expectations and communicated broadly.
3. Plan for fun and engagement. Fun is inspiring. Think themes, contests, awards, challenges. Plan to offer a word of encouragement whenever you go into war room strategy meetings, internal business reviews (IBRs), or out in the field with sellers.

Yellow and Red flags Alerts

Examples of Yellow Flags

- Sales leaders miss key account war room meetings and are distant from account teamwork.
- Account quarterback lacks inspiration and dedication.
- Account team lacks motivation, and account momentum is slowed.
- War room account strategy sessions are unproductive or primarily tactical.

Examples of Red Flags

- Account teams disband during the sales process.
- Prospect development is stalled.

Defensive Remedies

- Follow the best practices outlined in this Playbook.
- Use assessments to understand underlying motivators and styles for each account team member.
- Engage account teams in team development activities to build cohesion and teamwork early in the process.
- Bring in an outside facilitator, coach or consultant to help get the team back on track or diagnose core issues after the fact.

Play Models

**TOP LINE ACCOUNT™ PROGRAM
KICK OFF COMMUNICATION**

Date:

To: Account Team – War Room Participants

From: Executive Sponsor (internal)

You have been selected to serve on the X account team. This assignment comes with great responsibility as you will be working on expanding services within our largest customer. Our greatest priority is to grow revenues, and we believe that increasing revenue within our loyal customer base is the best way to achieve our goal.

The account team will begin by defining roles and responsibilities within the team as well coming to agreement on foundational elements such as commitment to the process, full participation and team play.

Please give this work your best creativity, problem solving and strategic thinking. Each account team member will bring a unique perspective, and everyone's contribution should be valued. We are counting on you to collaborate with your co-workers during regular war room meetings as you work through all the strategic elements necessary to achieve your short, medium and long term account goals.

I am also committed to this process and will be involved and available to move the account forward. I look forward to celebrating your small victories and large wins along the way.

ACCOUNT TEAM AGREEMENTS

Account Team Roles and Responsibilities

High Performing Account Team Roles	Sample of Division of Responsibilities	Account Team Roles & Responsibilities (who/what)
Executive Sponsor (Internal)	Account team expectations, inspiration, recognition, encouragement, resource deployment, issue resolution.	
Team Leader/Account Quarterback	Group facilitator, ensures full team participation. Leverages individual and team strengths.	
Team Communication	Account team communication methods and frequency, communication of important or timely action item completion.	
Team Challenger	Designated person who challenges the team's thinking including account strategy, goals and actions.	
Meeting Organizer	Initiates team discussion and gains agreement on essential content for war room agendas; decides on frequency, duration and format for meetings; schedules meetings.	

High Performing Account Team Roles	Sample of Division of Responsibilities	Account Team Roles & Responsibilities (who/what)
Account Document Repository	Strategy Brief; updates, version control, access and distribution–i.e. shared drive, CRM, external tool or application.	

Account Team Agreements

High Performing Account Team Agreement Areas	Sample of Agreements (customize for each team)	Account Team Agreements
War Room Attendance, Participation and Commitment	Make war rooms a priority, actively participate in discussions, and follow through on all commitments.	
Team Player	Be a team player, support fellow team members. Strong belief that the 'team gets it right' through healthy debate and discussion.	
Confidentiality	Maintain account war room confidentiality as well as Strategy Brief confidentiality.	
Team Dispute Resolution	Discuss issues openly within team. Discuss private issues with account team leader, executive sponsor or manager.	
Winning and Losing	Commit that the team will win and lose together. Celebrate wins and learn from losses. No blaming.	

Playbacks

Check the related Play #9 Designate and Enable the Account Quarterback.

Sideline Coach: Expert Opinion
Jay Tyler, CEO, Jay Tyler Consulting

I have had the pleasure of training and coaching at least 300 sales managers, directors, VPs and CROs per year for many years. In that time, I have learned how first line leaders want to be inspired by their sales leaders. Account teams are no different. Account teams are inspired by managers who spend their time focused on being effective rather than efficient. When 'must win' opportunities are at stake, effective managers concentrate on teaching account team members how to do what it takes to win. They create war rooms, coaching sessions and pre-call planning meetings on their calendar. They help craft emails, LinkedIn® communications and executive communications. They spend time making customer calls. They problem solve with the team instead of judging when longer term opportunities become stalled.

Most importantly, they figure out how to transfer their skills to their account team. They create an environment of positivity and willingness to do the hard work in order to close big opportunities. For truly big deals, they commit to staying involved with the account team from beginning to end.

Sadly, statistics paint a different picture. They paint a picture of frantic sales managers spending their time on late stage opportunities, chasing reps for inaccurate forecasting and thereby canceling out of field travel or important account strategy sessions. Their calendars, which should clearly demonstrate what's important, are out of control. Instead of intentionally taking the time to understand the root cause of their issues, they continue to spend their time reacting, leaving little time or energy to activate and inspire account teams. In short, sales leaders spend too much time on the *urgent* and not enough time on the *important*.

When I work with sales leaders, I start off with the sixteen global leadership competencies. Inspiration is the number one competency we want from our leaders. Yet, employees consistently rate their leaders last for their ability to inspire.

World class first, second- and third-line sales leaders focus on what's most important like early stage opportunity building. They intentionally block out time and commit to those activities associated with identifying, developing and closing really big accounts. They dig into the details and follow a proven process. They coach and strategize versus direct. They choose to be effective over being efficient. This commitment to sharing their best is truly inspirational for account teams.

PLAY #2

Establish 5X Deal Sales Expectations

"A goal is a dream with a deadline."

–NAPOLEON HILL

Play Attributes

Big deal expectations provide clarity for behaviors, actions, attitudes, approaches and results specific to identifying, developing and closing really large contracts. The purpose is to define a standard of excellence or paint the picture of what success looks like. These expectations will augment your general sales expectations.

Constructing the Play

- Sales leaders should approach expectations-setting sessions in a collaborative manner with sellers. Encourage sellers to clarify and ask questions and provide input. Transparency in developing joint expectations around big deals will yield the largest dividends.
- Leading the desired change will go a long way towards helping the account team members meet and exceed big deal expectations. For example, securing an

appointment with a hard to reach executive sponsor to show how it's done will have a memorable impact.

- Big deal expectations should include both process and results expectations. Process expectations might include number of accounts scored, number of war room sessions held, Strategy Brief completion, evidence of movement through the sales process, or other measurable criteria.
- Big deal expectations should be in writing and clear to all. Goals should be stated as SMART goals.
- Sales leaders should incorporate reinforcement and coaching through one-on-ones, forecasting sessions, field travel or before/after account war room sessions.
- Sales leaders should be constantly on the look-out for opportunities to recognize behaviors, actions, attitudes and results.
- Sales leaders must be aware of barriers to success. They should clear the way for sellers to be successful.

Deploying the Play

1. Develop clear expectations associated with:
   a. big deal prospect movement
   b. account team accountability
   c. momentum with agreed upon actions
   d. war rooms
   e. pre-call planning
   f. progress on strategic elements such as the pre-strategy SWOT, strategy charting, relationship mapping, competitive blocks deployed and use of other important tools included in the Advances sub-chapters
2. Schedule time to introduce and gain agreement on big deal sales expectations.
3. Include a review and reinforcement of big deal sales expectations on your agenda for your normal monthly meetings.
4. Refresh and document big deal sales expectations annually.

Yellow and Red Flag Alerts

Examples of Yellow Flags

- Sellers are not clear on big deal expectations.
- Sales managers set expectations but don't have a system to reinforce or recognize progress.
- Month to month sales expectations (i.e., 30-day mentality) are more important than big deal or longer-term sales expectations.
- Sales leaders don't provide one-on-one coaching or training opportunities for seller growth and development.

Examples of Red Flags

- Less than ideal feedback from customers or co-workers on sellers' skills and behaviors.
- Sub-standard results.

Defensive Remedies

- Follow the best practices outlined in this Playbook.
- Go back to the beginning to reset big deal expectations.
- Increase management attention including coaching and reinforcement of expectations.
- Diagnose performance issues to understand and address the root cause; for example, knowledge, skills, ability, attitude and desire.

Play Models

TOP LINE ACCOUNT™ SELLER EXPECTATIONS FOR 5X DEAL SUCCESS

Attitude and Approach

- Embody the company's mission and values with strategic (or major or global or national, etc.) customers and prospects.
- Maintain a positive, can-do attitude towards account development.
- Invest in personal growth and development for 5X deals on a regular basis.
- Generate enthusiasm with customer or prospects.
- Tackle problems and issues with a solution-oriented attitude. Bring ideas to the table.
- Think out of the box. Leverage all products and solutions available to customer or prospect.
- Show initiative.
- Help the account team to think strategically.
- Follow the '5X deal' methodology for each opportunity.
- Be ready to step out of your role to help team members, i.e., new account team members.
- Differentiate yourself and the company in the eyes of the prospect or customer.

Behaviors and Actions

- Manage and maintain account relationships, both high and wide.
- Engage executive sponsor (C-level) and ensure the executive sponsor's door remains open.
- Take the lead in scheduling war room meetings for the account team.
- Facilitate war room sessions to maximize account team productivity.
- Develop strategies and tactics for each strategic account or prospect.
- Maintain up-to-date account information, i.e., Strategy Brief.
- Clearly understand customer and prospect priorities, problems and requirements.
- Work with the account team to develop compelling Win Themes™.
- Maintain account visitation expectations.

Behaviors and Actions
Follow up on customer issues or requests within 48 hours, i.e., either resolution or progress report.
Communicate regularly with account team to ensure accountability for actions and momentum.
Tap into inside and outside resources for the benefit of the account or prospect.
Establish cross functional alliances within the company for the benefit of the customer.
Engage the account team in formal pre-call planning for all important customer meetings.
Understand customer and prospect's industries.
Collaborate with senior level company executives to execute on account plans.
Partner with key customers and prospects on plans and initiatives.
Execute on proactive account management programs such as annual executive reviews.
Use sales tools such as case studies effectively.
Use sales technology tools such as the CRM efficiently.

Results
Drive revenue and profit from strategic accounts.
Ensure customer satisfaction within strategic accounts.
Ensure account team engagement and ongoing accountability to results.
Be accountable for renewals and customer retention.
Be accountable for expansion of products and services by upselling or cross selling.
Move prospect from stage to stage in the complex opportunity sales process.

SIGNATURE   DATE

SIGNATURE   DATE

Playbacks

Check out the related Play #9 Designate and Enable the Account Quarterback.

Check out the related Play #12 Conduct Internal 5X Business Reviews.

Sideline Coach: Expert Opinion

Suzanne Paling, author of *The Sales Leader's Problem Solver* and *The Accidental Sales Manager* and Founder, Sales Management Services

When it comes to expectations setting for account teams, getting granular around prospect communications is a game changer. I'm reminded of a recent story. Talking with the President of a software company about his communications preferences, he said, "Please don't call me on my cell; I prefer to use my land line. I just naturally gravitate towards it. I keep my cell phone on my left and the land line on my right." You can bet that I never used his cell again.

Included in this Playbook is a tool for Relationship Mapping, and I would add one more aspect to that tool – contact communication preferences. In other words, asking each important contact on your Relationship Map how best to communicate with them? Do they prefer text, email, phone? Specific to decision makers, what would they like to be cc'd on?

It might even be good to ask what annoyances they have with any type or method of communications, i.e., lengthy emails, too many emails, using LinkedIn® for email, texting outside of work hours, etc. Once you've nailed down the communication ground rules for each contact, share with the entire account team so everyone is in compliance.

Periodically check in with the important contact to make sure this communication plan is working and that all other staff members are adhering to it. This takes little time and garners much appreciation. It showcases you as a professional who listens and pays attention to the details.

Big deals can go on for months or years and include many team members on both sides. So, setting an expectation with account team members to have positive and appropriate communications with each prospect contact will endear them to your company. If choosing between two closely matched vendors, they might select your organization.

PLAY #3

Create a Blueprint for Cross-Functional Collaboration

"Success is neither magical nor mysterious. Success is the natural consequence of consistently applying basic fundamentals."

–JIM ROHN

Play Attributes

Truly gargantuan contracts are won as a team. Account teams include resources from throughout your company so it's critical for sales leaders to build alliances early and often. Common alliances are Marketing, Sales Development and Customer Success, but depending on the opportunity, many other departments throughout the organization may add value to the account strategy and ultimately the contract closure. A perfect example is a Request for Proposal (RFP) that the company wants to win. It wouldn't be uncommon for the RFP team to include finance, legal, implementation, professional services, project management, company executives, technical resources, customer support and other subject matter experts (SMEs). The object of this Play is to engage all the correct players to form the account team.

Constructing the Play

- Sales leaders should work hard to develop positive relationships across the organization.
- The key to establishing cross-functional alliances is trust and communication.
- A balanced account team might include executive team representatives, marketing, technical/IT, customer service, business development or inside sales, legal, finance, manufacturing and other subject matter experts.
- Key account resource people should be included in strategic account training sessions so they understand the large opportunity development process.
- Account resources, people inside and outside the company, should be included in account war room meetings.
- Account team members can add the most value when brought in at the correct time with the right amount of background information.
- Exposing your customer or prospect to the depth of your account team can mitigate the customer or prospect's perceived risk of moving forward with your company.

Deploying the Play

1. Sales leaders should meet with their cross-functional counterparts and discuss the methodology associated with identifying and developing massive contracts.
2. Sales leaders should ask for support in terms of participation in account development activities such as war rooms, executive-to-executive programs and other prospect focused efforts.
3. The account quarterback or sales leader should facilitate a session on team agreements to include roles, communications, meetings and accountability.
4. Communications about account progress should occur proactively and regularly.
5. Sales leaders might engage in a dialog with company executives about providing a bonus for each account team member.
6. Sales leaders carry the ultimate responsibility for trust and cooperation among account team members and must monitor over time.
7. The entire account team should be included in the win celebration.

Yellow and Red Flag Alerts

Examples of Yellow Flags

- Account teams that only include sales.
- Initial cross-functional involvement in war room sessions that tapers off over time.
- Sales asking for help from others at the last minute, too late for them to add value.
- Lack of appreciation for cross-functional team member involvement.
- Failing to keep key account team members in the loop and informed.
- Account lead trying to keep all control, not facilitating a team-oriented approach.

Examples of Red Flags

- Resistance from other departments to engage in account development through war room sessions.
- Executives are too busy to form relationships with account executive sponsors.
- Dysfunctional account teams with members who undermine the process, resist, are unaccountable for action items, behave like rogues.
- Win celebrations that fail to include all the people who participated in the sales process.

Defensive Remedies

- Follow the best practices outlined in this Playbook.
- Engage in team building activities to set a baseline of cooperation as account teams are chartered.
- Use personality or style assessments to enhance cross functional collaboration.
- Expect account quarterback or sales leader to set clear expectations for account team roles.
- Have on-going sales leader check-ins and spot assessments of team effectiveness.
- Ensure sales leadership is proactively addressing all yellow and red flags versus assuming they will work out on their own.

Play Models

CROSS FUNCTIONAL COLLABORATION TEAM & RESOURCES PROMPTS

Executive sponsor (internal)	Account lead/quarterback
Sales leader	Account management
Technical resources	Professional services
Customer service	Customer success
Marketing	Inside sales/business development
Subject matter experts	Vendor partners/suppliers
Legal	Channel partners
Manufacturing	Research & development
Consultant (external)	Finance

Sideline Coach: Expert Opinion

Deb Calvert, President of People First Productivity Solutions and author of *DISCOVER Questions® Get You Connected* and *Stop Selling & Start Leading*

I would like to start with my definition of team effectiveness and that is, "The capacity a group of interdependent individuals has to accomplish their own and their shared goals and objectives." This definition green lights and makes it okay that we all have individual goals to reach at the same time we work together to achieve our shared goals. This approach minimizes internal competition. Teams are truly effective when they can see the shared vision and the obstacles preventing performance are cleared.

Account teams are generally temporary teams in that they come together temporarily for a project. The project might be an RFP response or a longer effort to identify, develop and close a big opportunity. At the core of a collaborative temporary team is trust. When teams have high trust, they will engage in healthy conflict. Even if they agree to disagree on an issue, the true commitment to the shared goal remains. Teams that lack trust or have a breach of trust might have team members who fake buy-in or have a mentality of "let's just get it over with." High trust teams perform and get results while dysfunctional teams tend to disintegrate quickly.

Establishing a foundation of trust and a shared vision begins with openly addressing any gaps or issues such as misalignment of goals. Discussion about roles and responsibilities, team charter, and development of shared goals are good trust builders. Team listening assessments can improve team and organizational communications.

High trust teams, especially temporary teams, need to know how to listen and understand each other. That's what translates into the shared commitment that wins big deals.

PLAY #4

Mentor and Develop Account Teams

"Management is about planning, organizing, staffing, directing and measuring. Leadership, on the other hand, is the ability to translate vision into reality. A leader does this through strategic thinking and honest communications, while inspiring and motivating others to be their best."

–KRISTA S. MOORE

Play Attributes

In the world of big deals, much of the coaching will be with the account team vs. individual sellers. However, super successful sales leaders will do both. The following definition can be applied to an individual or a team.

"Coaching is unlocking a person's potential to maximize their own performance. It is helping them to learn rather than teaching them."

–JOHN WHITMORE, COACHING FOR PERFORMANCE

There are volumes of books and materials on coaching, so for the purpose of this playbook, our entire focus is on the nuts and bolts of mentoring account teams, especially the account quarterback. The purpose of this play is for sales leaders to provide the right environment and correct support for the accounts teams to be successful.

Constructing the Play

- Sales leaders have two important mentoring roles:
  - Mentor and develop the account quarterback
  - Mentor and develop the account team
- Sales leaders should encourage and develop account quarterbacks to provide account team leadership. However, the sales leader must stay involved as the overall leader.
- The most effective big deal coaches understand the process and help account teams follow a proven methodology.
- Sales leaders should model the desired behaviors and actions until the skills are transferred and practices become habits.
- Sales leaders must be present by fully engaging in all aspects of the big deal process such as war room strategy sessions and pre-call planning for big meetings.
- Much of account team coaching is facilitating group discussion which can include disagreements. In the end, the account team usually gets it right. The sales leader's job is to facilitate healthy discussion, including debate, to that end.
- Big deal account teams require a mix of skills and abilities. It's important for sales leaders to have a clear understanding of what *good* looks like and pull the best from all team members.
- Team assessments can offer a baseline from which to grow. The assessment should answer the question, "Is the team a high performing team?"
- The rule of complimenting in public and correcting in private applies to account teams. If correction is needed for a single account member, that should be handled in private.
- Encourage accounts teams through informal and formal big deal recognition programs.

- Invest in training to promote growth and development. Invest in your big deal sellers, equipping them with the knowledge, resources and tools to be successful. Reinforce training and all new concepts through involved coaching.

Deploying the Play

1. Engage in team building at the beginning of the account development process. Outings, naming the team and maybe even some friendly competition among other account teams are appropriate.

2. Help the account team decide on team agreements. Agreements include rules for communication, meetings, behaviors, confidentiality and more.

3. Clearly define roles for the account team, including the sales leader and the account quarterback. See Advance #4: Agreeing on Team Guidelines.

4. Decide on an approach for on-going account team coaching, such as during account strategy meetings plus one-on-one with the account quarterback and other account team members. Don't leave it to chance.

5. Challenge the account team through inquisitive and thought-provoking questions.

6. Use assessments to monitor team progress.

7. Map out and invest in annual training for account teams and big deal sellers.

8. Commit to a training reinforcement plan to capitalize on all learning opportunities.

Yellow and Red Flag Alerts

Examples of Yellow Flags

- Account teams aren't moving forward or functioning well.
- The account quarterback is a maverick and prefers to work as a lone wolf versus a team player.
- The account quarterback/lead is control-oriented and hesitant to allow other teams members to engage.
- Account teams aren't following the Plays or best practices.

- Account team roles are unclear, which is causing confusion.
- Teams are concentrating on the short-term vs long-term strategic account planning.

Examples of Red Flags

- Big opportunities are stalled or aren't closing.
- Account teams are losing big deals.

Defensive Remedies

- Follow the best practices outlined in this Playbook.
- Diagnose the core of the dysfunction.
- Go back to the basics of team building, including team roles and team agreements.
- Assess the leadership skills of the account quarterback and provide focused coaching where needed.
- Re-visit the core team and resources document. The account team agreements document is a good tool to facilitate a positive discussion.
- Encourage teams to think broader. It helps to start with goals--long term account goals, medium term goals and short-term goals.
- Help teams follow the methodology. Systematically go back through all the strategy planning components and pre-call planning to improve close ratios. Encourage them to trust the process.
- Conduct extensive win/loss prospect retrospectives. Bring all learnings back to the account teams.

Play Models

TOP LINE ACCOUNT™ SALES LEADER 5X DEAL COACHING QUESTIONS

Identify

Where did the lead come from?

What do you know about them based on your initial research? (I.e., revenue, industry, leadership team (persona), business drivers, other research findings)

Did you uncover any common connections?

Do we have any history with this suspect?

Is this suspect part of an industry vertical where we have a foothold?

Where is the suspect in their buying process? (What are they doing, thinking, feeling?)

Can you walk me through the suspect's timeline?

Describe the suspect's need and any evidence of that need?

Have they involved others within their organization in the buying process?

What options do they see to solve their problem?

Why do you think we would be a fit?

How could other departments assist? What groups may be able to add value to this lead?

Is the opportunity solid enough to form an account team?

Have you considered all sales tools available at this stage and how you might use them?

Do you have a meeting set? (phone or in person)

Have you completed your pre-call plan?

What other actions have you taken?

What is your next step?

Have you added them to the CRM?

How can I help?

Qualify

Does this prospect share characteristics with any of your prior successes? Can you elaborate?

Does this prospect fit into an existing industry niche?

What insights have you developed based on your research?

Do you have evidence of the customer's pain points and their willingness and commitment to solve their problem?

Where is the prospect in their buying process? (How do you know?)

Can you describe the depth of knowledge we have gained in the following areas:
- Their requirements
- Priority of this project in relation to their other projects
- Decision makers (i.e., disposition, connections, authority)
- Decision process
- Timeline – why now?
- Budget
- Known barriers (i.e., political barriers, events, partnerships, contracts, relationships, competing priorities, options they are considering)

Why do you think we would be a good fit?

What are your initial Win Themes™? (I.e., intersection of the prospect's priorities and our strengths)

Is the prospect committed to the process through sharing of information and time?

What is the estimated value of the opportunity?

What is the estimated probability of close?

How could other departments assist? What groups may be able to add value to this prospect? Who is your internal executive sponsor?

Have you considered all resources and sales tools available?

Has the account team been engaged and war room meetings scheduled?

Has the opportunity been scored?

Have you started the Strategy Brief?

What actions have you taken?

Have your completed your pre-call plan for your next meeting?

What are your next steps?

Have you updated the CRM?

How can I help?

Develop

Where is the prospect in their buying process? (What are they doing, thinking, feeling?)

Have you met with the decision maker? (How long have they been the decision maker? How many times have they been involved with this decision process in the past?)

Are you helping the prospect drive their buying process?

Is the account team fully engaged?

How many elements of the Strategy Brief have been completed? Can we review?

What are your Win Themes™? (I.e., intersection of the prospect's priorities and our strengths)

Describe your understanding of their budget, timeline and decision-making process.

How often does this prospect go out for bid or source proposals?

How many proposals are they seeking?

Who are your competitors? How do you know?

What do we anticipate the competitor will do to position themselves with the prospect? What will we do to block?

Do any of the competitors have a prior relationship with the prospect? If yes, how will we overcome?

Do you have all the information you need to develop a proposal or quote?

What are their concerns at this point?

How could other departments assist? What groups may be able to add value to this prospect?

Have you considered all resources and sales tools available?

What actions have you taken?

Did they agree to a next step?

Are the appropriate members of the account team involved in pre-call planning for the next meeting?

Have you updated the CRM?

How can I help?

Propose

How did you involve the prospect in the proposal process?

Do you have a date/time to review the quote/proposal? (Do not send proposal without a meeting date to review.) Who will be in attendance?

Do you have all the information you need to finalize your proposal or quote?

Do they have enough information/value to make a decision in our favor? How do you know?

What are your Win Themes™? What evidence have you shared with the prospect to reinforce your Win Themes™?

Describe your understanding of their decision-making process after proposal delivery.

Has your main contact introduced you to others on the buying committee?

Can you confirm their timeline and procurement process?

What are their remaining concerns?

What are the competitors doing and proposing?

How could other departments assist? What groups may be able to add value to this proposal?

Have you considered all resources and sales tools available?

Is the account team fully engaged?

How many elements of the Strategy Brief have been completed? Can we review?

What is your account strategy and goals?

Did they agree to a next step?

Are the appropriate members of the account team involved in pre-call planning for the next meeting?

Have you updated the CRM?

How can I help?

Has the account team anticipated the following 'Late game' pitfalls? What have you done to address?

Possible Pitfalls

- Past trusted relationship uncovered
- Delays (I.e. Board meeting delay)
- No executive sponsor or executive sponsor nonresponsive
- New decision maker appears. (I.e. financial, IT or operational)
- Unresolved or new concerns
- Value not established
- Pricing negotiations
- New competitor emerges
- Unanticipated risk issues arise

Close – Win

Is the contract signed or do you have an appointment to get it signed?

Does the client have all the paperwork from us that they require?

Has the implementation plan been agreed to?

Have you lined up the proper implementation resources?

Do you have a date to do the win retrospective interview?

Have you thanked your internal champion or internal coach?

Do you have an internal meeting scheduled to share the learnings from the retrospective meeting?

Have you completed your pre-call plan to prepare for your next meeting?

Did you 'Ring the bell' sharing the good news?

Is a win celebration scheduled for the account team and resources?

Have you updated the CRM?

How can I help?

Close – Loss

Do you have a loss retrospective meeting set? (Don't forget pre-call planning for this interview. Needs to be customized.)

Do you have an internal team meeting set, following the customer retrospective, to share lessons learned?

Have you updated the CRM?

How can I help?

After internal and prospect loss retrospective

What did you learn from the loss retrospective?

Is there a next step?

Did you feel supported through this process?

How closely did you follow the sales process?

What stage of the sales process do you feel that we lost the opportunity?

Was there anything that you feel could have helped you to win?

What were the yellow flags identified during the sales process? How did the team attempt to resolve?

What will you do differently next time?

Expand

Is the customer satisfied with our products and services?

Did you ask if the customer would be willing to be a reference?

Did you ask for a referral?

Have you identified any expansion areas for our services?

If yes: Is the customer at the point where it is appropriate to cycle back to the qualify or develop stage?

Do you have a proactive account management plan in place?

Do you have a next meeting set with the customer?

Have you completed your pre-call planning?

Is the account team engaged and focused on expansion?

Do you have a plan to cultivate and continue to engage your executive sponsor?

Have you shared any important client updates or news with other divisions who might benefit?

Have you updated the CRM?

How can I help?

CAN WE WIN?
ACCOUNT TEAM ASSESSMENT

Purpose
- Temperature checks throughout the TOP Line Account™ journey will add a reality factor and keep the team on track
- Snapshots help the team to make necessary adjustments, at appropriate times, throughout the complex sales process
- Snapshot criteria should be customized for each opportunity to paint the most accurate picture

Can We Win Assessment

The goal of *Can We Win* snapshot is to assess the sales situation at important junctures throughout the complex sales process for 5X deals. By adding an objective measure through customized criteria, the team can discuss risk points and make needed adjustments.

Can We Win? Snapshot

Criteria	Response (Y/N)	Importance (1=Least, 10=Most)	Actions Needed
Is the prospect committed to solving their problem?			
Do you know the relative priority of your project in comparison to the other projects your prospect is considering?			
Can the prospect's requirements easily be translated into your product or service?			
Has your key contact made a decision in favor of your company in the past?			
Do you clearly understand the decision-making process and can you recount their buying criteria?			
Do you have an executive sponsor?			
Do you have an internal champion or coach?			
Are the lines of communication open between your selling team and the prospect's buying team?			
Do you have Win Themes™ that demonstrate your unique differentiators?			
Can you demonstrate evidence of cost savings, process improvements and customer satisfaction to the prospect?			
Have you set 'blocks' for your competitors?			
Would the prospect agree that your proposal represents a good overall value for their organization?			

TOP LINE ACCOUNT™ TRAINING REINFORCEMENT

Congratulations for investing in The TOP Line Account™ training program. To attain the results you're seeking, comprehensive reinforcement is necessary. New concepts and training require leadership support to yield desired changes. Below is a list of thought starters.

☑ Expect   ☑ Model   ☑ Encourage   ☑ Reinforce

Prior to Training

- Training sponsors and company leadership should consider the change path for participants (I.e., what does each individual need to make the changes required?)
- Pre-training written communications to attendees focusing on purpose of training, commitment and expectations for full participation. Generate enthusiasm!
- Encourage input and dialog on training objectives and agenda.
- Set expectation for results, outcomes or goals.
- Participant engagement prior to workshop such as:
  - pre-reading
  - homework
  - pre-training skill assessment

During Training Event

- Clear, compelling sponsor message (live or video) to kick off training or coaching program.
- Demonstrate commitment by management/leadership attendance and full (active and visible) participation.
- Include a *Participant Expectations* communication and ask attendees to review and sign.
- Expect management attendance at all reinforcement sessions.
- Take pictures or videos for future reinforcement.
- Share best practices and success stories to help promote concepts.
- Share success stories as a result of new skills, approaches, concepts.

Post Training - Immediate

- Send out post-training written recap of expectations for use of new approaches.
- Charter account teams. Designate and enable account quarterback/lead.
- Ask account quarterback/lead to set the first war room with their account teams.
- Publish a war room account strategy schedule and share with key stakeholders.
- Add use of new skills, approaches, processes and tools in individual job descriptions or MBO's.
- Hold attendees accountable for post-workshop programs such as personal action plans developed during training.
- Arrange buddy or accountability partner program.
- Manage post-training skill assessment.
- Appoint subject matter experts for important aspects of training/coaching skill areas.
- Set expectations for additional development such as recommended readings.
- Make training reinforcement a core agenda item for regular sales meetings.
- Create visible display of progress or results. (I.e. Wall of fame, leader board, ring the bell announcements)
- Set expectations for number of documented account strategy plans (i.e. Strategy Brief) or accounts scored.

Post Training – Day to Day

- Show leadership by using concepts, terms, tools and methodologies on a regular basis.
- Catch attendees in the "act of doing it right" and recognize them.
- Use sales management deal review coaching questions with account teams.
- Inspect what you expect through 1:1 encounters such as ride alongs, joint calls or pre-call planning.
- Continue executive messaging to strengthen initial expectations.

Post Training – Mid to Long Term

- Review pre-call planning work for all important TOP Line Account™ calls.
- Set regular deal review schedule.
- Engage second level managers for additional reinforcement.
- Provide regular written encouragement. (I.e., notes)

- Conduct 90/120/180+ day process checks or KPI's to measure progress and results. (Internal Business Reviews or IBRs)
- Solve any roadblock problems.
- Hold regular review and sharing sessions. (I.e., lunch and learns)
- Compile resources and tools to enhance learnings and make accessible to all. Update regularly. (I.e., Quick Reference Guide)
- Consider on-going communication vehicles to highlight successes, such as company or department newsletters.
- Commit and set criteria for win/loss customer retrospectives.
- Validate Win Themes™ prior to demos, presentations and RFP's.
- Create a certifciation program.
- Add training content (if licensed from trainer) to company LMS (Learning Management System) and CRM.
- Celebrate all TOP line account™ wins.
- Make it fun. (I.e., contests, use of photos or videos, games, use of humor, events)

Continue Expert Assistance

- Invest in follow-up reinforcement programs/coaching offered by trainer.
- Invest in war room strategy expert assistance offered by trainer for top account oportunities.
- Tap into trainer/coaches "spot reinforcement" programs such as newsletters.
- Schedule a reinforcement event within 6-12 months of initial training.
- Consider a Level II training to build on skills and keep momentum going.
- Expand ciriculum throughout your organization by investing in train the trainer programs offered through trainer, i.e., license content.
- Develop a customized Sales Leader Playbook for your organization to include training/skill reinforcement. (see templates available at *www.toplinesales.com*)

Playbacks

Check out the related Play #1 Inspire and Activate Account Teams.

Check out the related Play #3 Create a Blueprint for Cross-Functional Collaboration.

Check the related Play #9 Designate and Enable the Account Quarterback.

Sideline Coach: Expert Opinion
Krista S. Moore, author of *Race to Amazing: Your Fast Track to Sales Leadership* and Founder & CEO, K.Coaching, Inc.

I have three main points to add to the Play:
1. the most important aspects of the sales leader's role
2. the critical need for a problem resolution model
3. the responsibility of each account team member

Most Important Aspects of the Sales Leader's Role

The sales leader must lead through observation and coaching conversations especially with the account team quarterback. The leader sets the tone about the importance of the account team's work. A war room session is more than just a meeting; it's an opportunity to strategically work together as a team to transform the company. The leader should spark creativity and right brain possibilities. Leaders should draw out stories about past account successes and encourage members to share ideas and experiences.

The account quarterback should start each account strategy meeting by reminding the team of their value and how each member's role is critical to the overall success of the account. Their positive enthusiasm will be contagious and motivating, and in some cases this winning spirit will transfer to conversations between account team members and the prospect or customer. In this way, the leader has a strong teaching opportunity. If they role model listening, preparation and a consultative approach, account team members will mimic the same style.

Problem Resolution Model: Strong leaders constantly challenge the team and provide feedback. If account team members don't show up prepared and engaged or the team becomes dysfunctional in some way, the leader must step up to get things back on track. The best way to address team issues is through a problem resolution model. For example, if the team is struggling to make decisions, have a voting system. If a member is disruptive, have a predictable method to address. Anticipating the various issues that might arise within the account team and developing a clear model to address each issue will go far to advance the team's effectiveness.

It's an Honor to be selected for an Account Team: Each account team member should clearly understand that they are part of something big and have a strong purpose in their role. Members should be held in high regard by the account quarterback, sales leaders and other company leadership. The culture of the account team is that members were selected because they represent the best of the best. Account teams have an air of exclusivity, and it should be an honor to be part of such an important effort.

PLAY #5

Develop a 12-Month Cadence

*"We are what we repeatedly do.
Excellence, therefore, is not an act but a habit."*

—ARISTOTLE

Play Attributes

The 12-month calendar provides a snapshot of key sales leadership activities for the year. The snapshot enables sales leaders to anticipate, prepare and plan ahead. It also ensures that key activities aren't missed. The object of this play is for sales leaders to commit via their calendar to those critical success factors that contribute to winning 5X contracts repeatedly.

Constructing the Play

- Sales leaders should reference the calendar on a regular basis. It's a key planning tool.
- The Sales VP owns the 12-month calendar. Ownership includes initiating all important meetings and events.

Deploying the Play

1. The sales leadership team (direct reports to the Sales VP) should add all core meetings to their calendar at the beginning of the year.
2. The calendar should be shared with the broader sales organization to show them the big picture of events for the year and commitment to the 5X deal program.
3. Sales VPs should share the 12-month calendar with the executive team and key cross functional colleagues.
4. The 12-month sales leadership calendar should be refreshed each year during the planning process for the following year.

Yellow and Red Flag Alerts

Examples of Yellow Flags

- Lack of adherence to the calendar.
- Key events slip.

Examples of Red Flags

- Key activities are missed entirely.

Defensive Remedies

- Build the establishment and review of the calendar into other key management processes.
- Get buy-in and commitment to the calendar during the planning process.

Play Models

SALES LEADER: 12 MONTH CALENDAR SNAPSHOT

January	February	March
• Establish 5X deal expectations • Activate new account teams • Account war rooms (monthly) • Pre-call planning (monthly)	• Engage cross-functional resources • Set dates for 5X deal sales training program • Refresh or build executive outreach programs	• Internal 5X business reviews (IBRs) • Executive outreach activities • Coach account teams and quarterbacks • Win/loss retrospectives

April	May	June
• Account war rooms • Pre-call planning • Coach account teams and quarterbacks • Win celebrations	• 5X deal sales training conducted • Review executive outreach programs, adjust as necessary • 5X deal: system assessment	• Internal 5X business reviews (IBRs) • 5X deal sales training conducted • Win/loss retrospectives

July	August	September
• Account war rooms • Pre-call planning • Coach account teams and quarterbacks • Win celebrations	• 5X deal sales training conducted • 5X sales training reinforcement (change management) • Executive outreach activities	• Internal 5X business reviews (IBRs) • 5X deal sales training conducted • Win/loss retrospectives

October	November	December
• Account war rooms • Pre-call planning • Coach account teams and quarterbacks • Win celebrations	• Executive outreach activities • 5X sales training reinforcement (change management) • 5X deal: system assessment	• Final sales division goals and planning including training priorities for next year • Internal 5X business reviews (IBRs) • Win/loss retrospectives

PART TWO

Sales Methodology Plays

"Unless you try to do something beyond what you have already mastered, you will never grow."

–RALPH WALDO EMERSON

In this Part

5X Deal Sales Methodology Means…

- Committing to a strategic opportunity model
- Following all Advances
- Ramping up your sales process for complex opportunities
- Developing competitive block strategies

Sales Leader Interview Findings

Top Line Sales, January 2019

I completed over 40 hours of live interviews with 41 Sales VP between February and October 2018. Among the findings was this: **Challenges Overwhelm Priorities**

Sales leaders' #1 goal is achieving the revenue plan. In total, the sales leaders identified 24 unique priorities.

Conversely, they listed 51 unique challenges, about twice that of priorities.

The impact: sales leaders are bogged down by their numerous challenges, leaving limited time to help sellers with their big deals.

Part Two: Sales Methodology Plays addresses this issue.

Take your team to the next level by creating your custom **Sales Leader Playbook**:

Downloadable templates make it easy for your sales leadership team to build your own unique approach to leadership, methodology, execution and culture for a 5X deal generating sales organization. No need to start from scratch. Customizable templates available at *www.toplinesales.com*.

PLAY #6

Commit to a Strategic Opportunity Model

*"You were born to win, but to be a winner,
you must plan to win, prepare to win, and expect to win."*

–ZIG ZIGLAR

Play Attributes

The term "methodology" means a body of methods and rules: a particular procedure or set of procedures. (Source: Merriam-Webster)

For example, The TOP Line Account Way™ methodology is a way of doing things, much like a formula or system. The system includes a strategic framework based on a philosophy and supported by tools. This proprietary methodology helps account-based sales teams to identify, assess, advance, close and expand truly large opportunities. The purpose of committing to a strategic opportunity model is to turn every account team member into a strategic thinker and doer.

Constructing the Play

- Sales leaders and their teams must decide on a methodology, such as The TOP Line Account Way™ that's unique to large, complex accounts.
- The methodology should be comprehensive and detailed. It should include a philosophy consistent with a 5X deal sales culture, sales leadership approach, big deal development and vehicles for execution, i.e., tools.
- The methodology and tools must be separate and distinct from your normal sales process, for example, sales stages rather than steps. But at the same time, there should not be any points of conflict with your normal sales process.
- The methodology should support both new customer acquisition (new logos) and existing customer expansion (new revenue streams within an existing account).
- It's extremely helpful if your 5X methodology is supported by a solid technology platform. Most popular Customer Relationship Management systems (CRMs) are a good base, but 5X deals are best developed with additional applications that are integrated within your CRM.

Deploying the Play

1. Sales leadership team selects a methodology. Once a 5X opportunity is identified, the account team should follow the methodology to increase their chance of success. For example, The TOP Line Account Way™ model includes:
    a. Scoring opportunities
    b. Gathering insights
    c. Identifying and deploying the team and resources
    d. Mapping relationships
    e. Constructing a pre-strategy SWOT matrix
    f. Charting strategy
    g. Engaging executives
    h. Finding expansion opportunities
    i. Tracking progress
2. Sales leader monitors the elements and progress during internal business reviews (IBRs), war rooms and account calls. Each strategic planning activity yields

new and important information, which is put into action. When the account team commits to following all the steps, which usually occur over months or even years, they put themselves in the best position to win.

3   Sales leadership schedules opportunities to put the methodology into action. War rooms are practical evidence of a thriving methodology in action. War rooms and other evidence, such as large opportunity pre-call planning, executive communications, exec to exec programs, win retrospectives and win celebrations, should be occurring and visible on a regular basis.

Yellow and Red Flag Alerts

Examples of Yellow Flags

- Account teams all follow a different process to identify, develop, close and expand truly large opportunities.
- Sales leaders and managers lack a system to reinforce and recognize progress.
- Account teams aren't aware of or don't use the tools available to them.

Examples of Red Flags

- There is no evidence of the methodology in action through war rooms, large opportunity pre-call planning, executive communications, exec to exec programs, win retrospectives or win celebrations.
- Big deal results are lackluster or not predictable.

Defensive Remedies

- Follow the best practices outlined in this Playbook.
- Set clear expectations for following the methodology.
- Conduct seller training on your chosen methodology.
- Offer sales leader training and ongoing coaching on your chosen methodology.
- Keep sales leaders active and involved and provide regular account team mentoring.
- Put key activities, such as account war rooms, on the calendar in advance.

Playbacks

Check out the related Play #7 Ramp up your Sales Process for Complex Opportunities.

Play Models

THE TOP LINE ACCOUNT WAY™

5X Deal: Sales Success System Score Card

Culture		
Component	Score	Notes
Build a 5X Deal Sales Culture		
Establish Executive Outreach Norms		
Celebrate 5X Wins Across the Organization		
Define Repeatable Best Practices		

Leadership		
Component	Score	Notes
Inspire and Activate Account Teams		
Establish 5X Deal Expectations		
Create Cross-Functional Collaboration		
Mentor and Develop Account Teams		

Execution		
Component	Score	Notes
Designate and Enable Account Quarterbacks		

Execution		
Component	**Score**	**Notes**
Install Pre-call Planning Acumen		
Mobilize War Rooms		
Conduct Internal 5X Business Reviews		

Methodology		
Component	**Score**	**Notes**
Commit to a Strategic Opportunity Model		
Deploy Advances		
Ramp up Sales Process		
Develop Competitive Blocks		

THE TOP LINE ACCOUNT WAY™

5X Deal: Advances Score Card

Initiate		
Component	**Score**	**Notes**
Scoring opportunities		
Gathering insights		
Assigning team & resources		
Agreeing on team guidelines		

Develop		
Component	Score	Notes
Mapping relationships		
Constructing a pre-strategy SWOT matrix		
Charting strategy		
Designing Win Themes™		

Refine		
Component	Score	Notes
Designate and Enable Account Quarterbacks		
Install Pre-call Planning Acumen		
Mobilize War Rooms		
Develop competitive blocking strategies		

Expand		
Component	Score	Notes
Engaging executives		
Finding expansion opportunities		
Conducting customer business reviews		
Tracking progress		

5X DEAL: SALES SUCCESS SYSTEM

Scoring Guide

0-2 No process or practices in place. No results.

3-5 Scarce process or practices in place. Few results.

6-8 Coming up the learning curve. Hit or miss process or practices in place. Sporadic results.

9-10 Expertise is pervasive. Practice is a habit. Consistent results.

Thought Starters for Next Steps

1. Where are the biggest gaps in the assessment? How can we move the dial? (Think short term and long term.)
   a. What are the root causes of the gaps? – i.e. knowledge, skills, desire or ability to change
   b. What we should: start doing, stop doing, continue doing?
   c. Are there elements that will have a multiplier impact on our organization? i.e. war rooms or pre-call planning
2. Set next milestone meeting to gauge progress and update action plan.

Sideline Coach: Expert Opinion

Barbara Weaver Smith, Ph.D., Founder & CEO, The Whale Hunters and author of *Whale Hunting: How to Land Big Sales and Transform Your Company* and *Whale Hunting with Global Accounts*.

Sales VPs must understand the subtle differences between their standard sales process and a complex sales process. A standard sales process tends to be linear with steps, stages or phases all following a specific direction. A complex sales process is rarely linear and doesn't always follow a chronological timeline. It's messy and long. Many times, you have to go back to move forward. It can't be shoehorned into a normal sales process, or you run the risk of short circuiting the account team's efforts. Following a strategic opportunity model or system, which is flexible in nature, is the best way to navigate through the turbulent waters of large opportunity selling.

A few thoughts on the Advances included in the Playbook:

Gathering insights: Gathering insights is the most important work of the account team. It should be done repeatedly throughout the process. The initial research phase is an excellent time to engage your internal executive sponsor(s). They may have invaluable insights to share. As the various members of account team are checking multiple sources for information, they should share and discuss their findings with the entire account team. It's common for account executives to wonder why they have to gather so much information. However, it's only by sharing information through the collective minds of the account team that it will turn into knowledge. Account teams should not rush this step. Their learnings should include information about the prospect's industry, trends in that industry, current events and more. Many organizations spend most of their time talking internally and welcome the opportunity for an external perspective. If the account team can bring their prospects or customers insights on how their solution ties to company strategy, prospects will be interested in listening.

Team and Resources: Sales VPs must think about how they want the account team to work together. It should be part of the corporate culture for SMEs to participate in war room work. Companies shouldn't skimp on CRM access, especially for extended account resources. It's very motivating if account teams have a shared bonus or team comp associated with closing big contracts.

Expansion: Within the Advance: Finding Expansion Opportunities, the Sales VP should give some careful thought as to who is responsible for expansion opportunities. Who is assigned the revenue budget and who receives the compensation? What are the expectations around the various relationships required? Many times, especially with extremely large accounts such as global accounts, the lines are blurred. Here are three common scenarios:

Scenario #1: Account Executive - AE (or NAM or GAM) is responsible for expanding offerings within the account.

Upside: AE has 100% responsibility for revenue. No role confusion.

Downside: AE is distracted with firefighting issues. Customer treats them like a customer service representative and it's difficult for the AE to break out of this mode. As a matter of fact, the problem solver mode can be rewarding in that the customer is constantly offering praise and recognition for a job well done. The result – missed revenue opportunities.

Potential Solution: Set expectation for AE to engage the full account team around scoring for new opportunities and using the Finding Opportunities Advance every six months.

Scenario #2: Add an Account Manager (AM) to the account, assisting the Account Executive.

Upside: More people spotting new revenue opportunities. More people asking how to improve customer satisfaction. More people asking themselves what else can be done within the account.

Downside: If the program structure isn't crystal clear, there will be role confusion and blurred lines of responsibility. Having two or more resources engaged at the account level can also lead to communications issues.

Potential Solution: Call the AM a Project Manager to avoid confusion around the sales aspect of the job. The AE is responsible for sales; the PM is responsible for client services, including firefighting.

Scenario #3: Hand-off the account to an AM after the initial contract is closed.

Upside: AM has 100% responsibility for expansion revenue. No role confusion.

Downside: Can be disruptive for the customer if they have a strong relationship with the AE. Also, key information and coverage can be lost in the transition. In terms of generating sales, AM might be most comfortable with problem solving versus identifying and developing opportunities. AM's most common relationship is with the day to day contact and therefore the AM may not be as comfortable developing other key relationships including an executive sponsor.

Potential Solution: Set expectation for AM to engage the full account team to score for new opportunities and use the Finding Opportunities Advance every six months.

Advance One: Scoring Opportunities

"The man on top of the mountain didn't fall there."

–VINCE LOMBARDI

TOP Line Account™ Scoring Opportunities

Identifying the best candidates for TOP Line Account™ focus should include a well-rounded set of criteria. The example below includes definitions for your assessment and scoring. However, each sales organization should customize or develop their own criteria. Scoring will help you decide if the opportunity warrants the extra attention and focus associated with TOP Line Account™ strategy planning. Scoring is one of the most important elements of The TOP Line Account Way™.

Why Score?

- Scoring ensures account teams and sales leaders are getting the highest ROI on their time.
- Comprehensive scoring helps account teams focus on account opportunities with the highest likelihood of success.
- Scoring promotes critical thinking about top opportunities which helps avoid stalls and stops during the sales process.
- Scoring allows you to build your back up accounts which can be worked to move towards top opportunities in the future.

Sample Scoring Criteria and Definitions

Criteria	Definition
Financial Value	Estimated value of the opportunity is significant. (I.e. at least 5x your average contract size)
Strategic Value	The opportunity represents a strategic value for your company. Examples of strategic value might include: • a marquee name which would attract other customers • a desirable geography that your company is trying to break into • bolstering a division with the company through a big win • retaining an existing high profile or highly desirable customer

Criteria	Definition
Fit	Factors associated with fit generally include: • prospect's or customer's needs are a good match for your products or services • cultural alignment • vertical focus • geography is covered by your company • desirable financial disposition of prospect
Access	The selling team has access to key decision makers, influencers and stakeholders and access to internal company resources to execute on the account strategy.
Complexity	Complexity factors can include (but not limited to): • number of people involved in the sales process (your company and prospect) • customer perceived (or real) risk in making a change • anticipated length of sales process • political issues • geography • anticipated scope of services • number and intensity of competitors **Note: the higher the complexity, the higher the rating. Complex opportunities benefit from the process.**
Prospect/ Customer Commitment	The commitment of the customer to solve their problem and go through the buyer's journey all the way through closure.
Account Team Commitment	The commitment of the account-based selling team to dedicate the time and attention required to develop and close the opportunity. Consider any yellow flags such as account quarterback/lead is a Maverick and doesn't buy into a team approach, access to internal resources who will commit to the account team, or unique situation (i.e. geography) that means all relationships or action items fall to one member of the team.

TOP Line Account™ Score Card

Account Name: **Date:**

Opportunity Criteria	Criteria Rating (1 Low – 5 High)	Multiplied By	Importance Factor (1 Low – 3 High)	= Score
Financial Value		X		
Strategic Value		X		
Fit		X		
Access		X		
Complexity		X		
Prospect/Customer Commitment		X		
Account Team Commitment		X		
			TOTAL SCORE	

Scoring Notes: **Scoring Guide:**

75-105 = Excellent account choice for TOP Line Account™ system

50-75 = Account would benefit from applying the TOP Line Account™ system

Less than 50 = Consider proceeding with normal sales process

Advance Two: Gathering Insights

"When selling, you don't need a great answer, you do need a great question."

—ALICE KEMPER, 30-MINUTE SALES MEETINGS

Purpose

- Customer and prospect insights can only be gained through focused research.
- Effective research ensures solid preparation for all customer interactions.
- Gathering the right information will set you apart from the competition and accelerate your sales process.
- Customers don't have the time to answer basic questions that could have been answered easily through pre-work.
- You must gather insights at the company level and at the level that you work with day-to-day (business area level) to gain a holistic view.

Research Overview

Everyone agrees that it's important to conduct research prior to making sales calls and during strategic account planning. However, what research? How much depth is important? How should the information be used and shared?

The Goldilocks Principle

The Goldilocks philosophy of "Not too much, not too little, but just right" yields the most effective research approach and subsequent gathering of important insights. Here's how it works:

1. COLLECT	2. ORGANIZE
• Vision, mission, values • Priorities (goals, objectives, targets, initiatives) • Challenges (theirs) • Competitors (theirs) • Markets (trends) • Customers (theirs) • Company news • Industry news • History • Personal details related to your contacts • In other words, what's important to them?	**Company Level Intelligence:** • Their company-level priorities • Commonality between your organization and theirs • TOP level contacts and persona info **Business Area Level Intelligence:** • Projects/priorities • Problems you can solve • Areas you can impact • Immediate level contacts: Common connections/info about key contacts
3. FILTER	**4. APPLY**
Company Level Intelligence: • TOP company priorities • TOP alignment points between your company and theirs (Commonality) • TOP level contacts • TOP areas you can impact **Business Area Level Intelligence:** • TOP details about target contacts • TOP projects/priorities • TOP insights to engage your prospect • TOP things you want to learn more about	• Pre-call planning: review and recheck before all sales calls • Use insights gained during prospect interactions • Win Theme™ design • Share during account war room sessions • Update your account files/CRM

Key Insights from Research

Company Level Intel

Business Area Level Intel

Executive Summary

About:

Potential Value:

Current Products/Services Used:

Competition:

Other:

Internal Risk Assessment

Analyze the risk and return on investment for your sales efforts

- Do you have the resources to compete?
- Are you in a position to win?
- Are the investments of people, time and money worth the return (I.e. R & D)?
- Can you support this business over the long term?
- List any 'show stoppers':

Note your risk mitigation measures if applicable

Advance Three: Assigning Team and Resources

"It's hard to beat a person who never gives up."

—BABE RUTH

Purpose

- Identifying the core selling team and account resources early saves time later.
- Customers appreciate value-added resources.
- Team members can add the most value when brought in at the correct time with the right amount of background information.
- Depth of customer-facing resources can mitigate the customer's perceived risk of moving forward.

Team and Resources Overview

The goal of the Sales Account Team and Resource List is to identify all the people who can add value to developing and closing the opportunity. By identifying the core team and resources early in the sales process, those account related team members can be kept in the loop and be up to speed when they're needed. Successful account leaders are those who utilize all their resources at the right time in the sales process. Account team members can only be effective if they understand their role in the overall account strategy and have allocated time to assist.

Common Pitfalls

- Account lead wants solo control vs. a team approach
- Thinking too narrowly about members of the account team
- Asking for help at the last minute
- Failing to keep key resources in the loop and informed
- Lack of appreciation for support
- No agreement that account roles may be different than company titles

Points of Engagement

- Core selling team
- Just in time expertise
- As needed resources

Account Team and Resources

Team Member/Resource	Account Team Role	Point of Engagement	Notes

Account Team Roles

- Account Team Leader/Quarterback
- Sales Management
- Executive Team (Internal Executive Sponsor)
- Technical Resources
- Customer Service/Support
- Marketing
- Professional Services
- Subject Matter Experts (internal or external)
- Partners/Vendors/Suppliers (external)
- Legal/Finance
- Reference Sources (external)
- Consultants (external)
- Someone to Challenge the Team's Thinking (internal or external)

Point of Engagement

Core selling team, JIT expertise, and other needed resources.

Advance Four: Agreeing on Team Guidelines

*"Learn from the mistakes of others.
You can't live long enough to make them all yourself."*

—ELEANOR ROOSEVELT

Purpose
- Role clarity leads to high performing teams.
- Consensus on basic team responsibilities and agreements ensures teams run efficiently.
- Clear agreements help teams avoid common pitfalls.

Team Agreement Overview

The goal of account team agreements is to make sure that the entire account team is on the same page with regard to meetings, general communications and other aspects of effective team performance. This step is essential to set up the account team for success and should not be skipped or taken lightly.

Common Pitfalls
- Lack of clarity around team leader/quarterback and their responsibilities
- Weak account team quarterback
- Ineffective account team and resource communications
- Failure to keep account visibility high and moving forward
- Lack of accountability to action item completion
- Team and resources not engaged or too busy for proper account strategy planning work
- Lack of an internal executive sponsor

Account Team Roles and Responsibilities

High Performing Account Team Agreements	Sample of Agreements (customize for each team)	Account Team Agreements (what)
War room attendance, participation and commitment	Make war rooms a priority, actively participate in discussions, and follow through on all commitments.	
Team player	Be a team player, support fellow team members. Strong belief that the 'team gets it right' through healthy debate and discussion.	
Confidentiality	Maintain account war room confidentiality as well as Strategy Brief confidentiality.	
Team dispute resolution	Discuss issues openly within team. Discuss private issues with account team leader, executive sponsor or manager.	
Winning and losing	Commit that the team will win and lose together. Celebrate wins and learn from losses. No blaming.	

Account Team Agreements

High Performing Account Team Agreements	Sample of Agreements (customize for each team)	Account Team Agreements (what)
War room attendance, participation and commitment	Make war rooms a priority, actively participate in discussions, and follow through on all commitments.	
Team player	Be a team player, support fellow team members. Strong belief that the 'team gets it right' through healthy debate and discussion.	
Confidentiality	Maintain account war room confidentiality as well as Strategy Brief confidentiality.	
Team dispute resolution	Discuss issues openly within team. Discuss private issues with account team leader, executive sponsor or manager.	
Winning and losing	Commit that the team will win and lose together. Celebrate wins and learn from losses. No blaming.	

Advance Five: Mapping Relationships

"A little progress each day adds up to big results."

−SIMPLESUCCESSPLANS.COM

Purpose

- Identify all the necessary relationships within the account
- Break down the strategies of interacting with critical account contacts
- Align selling team members with account contacts with a clear goal based on the disposition of each contact

Relationship Map Overview

The goal of mapping relationships is to chart key relationships by assessing each contact and pairing him or her with the most appropriate resource in your organization. Based on the mapping and assessment, the selling team can develop next steps and tactics to deepen relationships and achieve account goals. The number of relationships you will need is growing, especially for large opportunities. Consider the need for an executive sponsor, the decision maker, influencers, subject matter experts, stakeholders, end users and an internal champion or coach.

Account Contact	Position (Title)	DMR	SP	PI	Coverage	Relationship Goals

Note: Many times, a single person can have multiple roles.

Decision-Making Role (DMR)	Strategic Position (SP)	Political Influence (PI)	Coverage
(D) Decision Maker	(P) Promoter	(H) High	Primary and secondary persons to build and maintain the customer relationship.
(R) Decision Ratifier	(N) Neutral	(M) Medium	
(I) Decision Influencer/SME	(T) Threat or Nemesis	(L) Low	
(U) Unknown	(U) Unknown	(U) Unknown	

Internal Relationship Questions

1. What do we know about each contact?
2. What did we uncover during our research?
3. What is their Persona and/or Style? (i.e., analytical, technical, social, driver, reserved, etc.) How will we adjust based on this knowledge?
4. What are their interests?
5. How long have they been in their job?
6. Have they done any similar projects in the past? Purchased a product or service similar to ours? If so, what was the result?
7. What is their political influence? How do we know?
8. How are they compensated or motivated? What would make them look good internally?
9. What are their goals? What aspect of our project will impact their goals?
10. What is their preferred communication method? i.e., email, text, phone or other
11. What is our plan to cultivate the relationship?

Sample Customer or Prospect 'Nuts & Bolts' Questions

1. Have you considered your internal team and their roles in this project?
   a. Key stakeholders, e.g., IT, key departments
   b. End users

    c   SMEs, e.g., legal, finance, procurement

    d   Decision makers and ratifiers

    e   Executive sponsor(s)

2. Is there anyone else in the organization who will be involved with this contract, e.g., implementation team?

3. Who are the core team members who will have ownership post-implementation? (For example, IT, operations, marketing, etc.)

4. Is there anyone within the organization who might not look favorably on this project?

5. What is the best way to connect your executive sponsor with our executive sponsor? Can you help facilitate a meeting?

6. What relationships do our competitors currently have in place?

7. Who will sign our agreement?

Advance Six: Constructing A Pre-Strategy SWOT Matrix

*"Whatever got you where you are today
is no longer sufficient to keep you there."*

–STEPHEN E. HEIMAN, CO-AUTHOR OF *STRATEGIC SELLING*

Purpose

- Precursor to developing account strategy and goals
- Provides team clarity by mapping elements
- Methodology drives strategic thinking
- Analyzes current situation from prospect's or customer's point of view

Pre-Strategy Overview

The goal of the Pre-Strategy SWOT Matrix is to diagram all the known strategic elements prior to developing the sales strategy and goals. The selling team should update the Pre-Strategy SWOT Matrix frequently and referred to it often throughout the sales process. It's a good early step once a TOP Line Account™ opportunity is identified and scored. This Matrix is a foundational element of the account strategy planning methodology.

PRE-STRATEGY 'SWOT' MATRIX

Strategic Points of Strength	Strategic Points of Weakness
INTERNAL	INTERNAL
EXTERNAL	EXTERNAL
Strategic Opportunities	Threats
	INTERNAL
	EXTERNAL

Switching Costs?

Matrix Considerations

1. What does the customer view as your strong points? Weak points?
2. What opportunities does the account team see to move your position forward?
3. What threats does the team see to moving forward? (Threats can include your competition or any option that your customer has to solve their problem including a choice to do nothing.)
4. Regarding "switching costs" or "non-preferred vendor costs":
   a. How do they affect all four quadrants? For example, are there political or strategic costs associated with switching providers?
   b. What are the operational or capital costs associated with a change?
   c. What other "pain of change" issues might the customer identify, and do these issues represent a strength or a threat to your strategy?
   d. What is the least path of resistance for the customer? If this path isn't your solution, then it represents a threat to your success.

Translate Pre-Strategy SWOT into Actions

What are the action items (Tactics) and who owns the actions to accomplish the following?

1. Build on points of strength?
2. Minimize points of weakness?
3. Capitalize on opportunities?
4. Neutralize threats?

Advance Seven: Charting Strategy

"The secret of victory lies not in defeating the enemy, but in defeating the enemy's strategy – therein lies their vulnerability."

–SUN TZU, THE ART OF WAR

Purpose

- A well-crafted strategy keeps the selling team focused on what's most important.
- Breaking down strategic components into smaller elements helps drive goal attainment.
- Strategy charting turns the entire account team into strategic thinkers and doers.

Strategy Charting Overview

The aim of Strategy Charting is to develop clear account strategies, goals and tactics. Strategy charting is also a good time to consider (or re-consider) your internal risk assessment.

Strategy CHARTING Definitions	
Strategies	Strategies are high-level objectives that define your priorities and help you set your goals. Strategy statements might begin with "Our strategy is to *introduce, expand, multiply, concentrate or replicate.*" Strategy = What.
Goals	Goals are specific objectives you're trying to accomplish. They should be clear, measurable and time-bound. (that is, SMART goals) Each strategy should have one or more goals. It's important to have a mix of short-term goals, mid-term goals, and long-term goals. The account team should define the timeframes associated with short, mid- and long-term as it relates to goals.
Tactics	Tactics are the action items that help you achieve your goals and realize your strategy. They are the HOWs.

Strategy Charting Steps

Use the Strategy Chart to develop clear account strategies, goals, and Win Themes™. Reference the Pre-Strategy SWOT Matrix.

Strategies: High-level objectives that define your priorities and help you set your goals. For example, "Our strategy is to expand, replicate, introduce or multiply."

Goals: Goals should help you achieve your strategy. State goals as SMART goals.

Key Strategies or Strategic Initiatives

Test your strategy

- Is your strategy consistent with your customer's or prospect's priorities?
- Is your strategy action oriented?
- Does your strategy comprehend any customer-perceived risks such as political influences or the pain of change?
- Is the entire account team aligned with your strategy?
- How will your competitors respond to your strategy?

Set your goal or goals (focus on critical few)

Short Term Goal(s)

_____

Medium-Term Goal(s)

_____

Long-Term Goal(s)

_____

Now, test your goals

_____

- Are your goals specific, measurable, actionable, reasonable?
- Is the timeframe achievable?

More on Goals

- Is your goal a SMART goal: specific, measurable, actionable, reasonable and time-bound?
- When you set your goal, did you consider the potential roadblocks, i.e., availability of resources, dependencies, etc.?
- Is the path clear to achieve your goal?
- Do you have systems in place that support the path to achieve your goals?
- Do you have control over most of the variables to attain your goal?
- Are you (and the account team) accountable to your goal(s)? Does the team really own it? If not, what can you do?
- Are you tapping into all your resources?
- Are account goals visible and driving actions and behaviors towards achievement?
- Are you measuring progress and making necessary adjustments?
- Are you on track to accomplish your goals? If not, do you have a 'Plan B'?
- Is the impact of achieving your account goals helping the team to stay focused and motivated?
- Does the selling team know the consequences of failing to achieve account goals?
- Can the team visualize the feeling of success when they accomplish the goals? (Think prior 'Win' celebrations.)

Advance Eight: Designing Win Themes™

"It's better to know some of the questions than to know all of the answers."

—JAMES THURBER

Advance Attributes

Win Themes™ are the intersection points between your prospect's priorities and the strengths of your offering. They are always prospect specific. They're the top three to four areas of overlap which ensure alignment between you and your prospect. They go well beyond your product or service offering. They

- differentiate your company,
- focus your sales conversations on the highest value areas,
- create receptivity for your products and services, and
- block your competitors.

WIN THEMES™
A client specific value proposition

Prospect's Priorities — WIN THEMES™ — Your Company's Strengths

Constructing the Advance

Sales leaders must understand Win Themes™ to help account teams maintain focus on prospect priorities and alignment. Sales leaders should also be able to articulate the difference between prospect-specific Win Themes™ and the concepts/tools below which are similar but different.

- Value Proposition
- Elevator Pitch
- Differentiation Points
- Features and Benefits

Once the account team designs the Win Themes™, they can determine what evidence will support each Win Theme™. For example,

Evidence for Win Themes™

- References, quotes, testimonials, case studies, examples
- Results–charts, dashboards, white papers, statistics
- Third party endorsements
- Stories
- Demos, tours, customer evaluations, pilot programs

Why Is Evidence Important?

- Evidence substantiates your claims.
- Evidence is remembered.
- Evidence is believable because it is concrete.

Sales leaders and account quarterbacks should help the account team refine Win Themes™ regularly, especially after new information is uncovered.

Having someone challenge the account team's thinking is also very powerful.

Sales leaders must also ensure that Win Themes™ are used for pre-call planning, demos, presentations, executive summaries or any other high-impact prospect interaction.

Account teams should reinforce Win Themes™ throughout the sales process.

Deploying Win Themes™

- As a key part of pre-call planning
- Throughout customer conversations and communications
- To enhance a demo or presentation
- Within a proposal (Including RFPs)
- The Theme of your executive summary

Advance Model for Win Theme™ Development

Describe your prospect's priorities	Why is this priority important to your prospect?
1	1
2	2
3	3
4	4

Describe your strengths specific to your prospect's priorities	Evidence
1	1
2	2
3	3
4	4

Win Theme™ Phrases or Sentences

Win Themes™ are best communicated as short sentences that articulate your customized, customer or prospect specific, value proposition. Always start with your prospect's priorities when talking about Win Themes™.

Messages should be reinforced 5-7 times to be remembered.

Brainstorm an inventory of phrases or sentences that reinforce your Win Themes™:

- **Example:** We understand your priority of X and will support you with X, Y and Z. For example, …
- **Example:** We are committed to X which will address your goal of X. As a point of reference, we …
- **Example:** In order to facilitate your objective of X, we will … The impact of this approach will be X, Y and Z. We have used this same approach with X, and the results were …

Sample Sales Questions to Uncover Customer Priorities

1. What are your biggest priorities (objectives, goals, initiatives, projects) for this year? Next 2-3 years?
2. What are the top priorities of your company's senior leadership team?
3. How do your short-term goals compare to your long-term goals?
4. Where are most of your resources (people, time, financial, tools) focused this year?
5. Has your team placed any weightings on your priorities or challenges?
6. What underlying drivers are most affecting your priorities or challenges?
7. How are current challenges affecting your business? What will happen if these challenges aren't addressed?
8. What would be the biggest benefits to your business if you addressed this problem (or opportunity) area?
9. Several of our other clients in your industry are focused on X; is this a priority for you as well?
10. Would a good summary of your most important focus areas be X?

Sideline Coach: Expert Opinion
Lisa Dennis, author of Value Propositions that Sell and Founder & President, Knowledgence

As it relates to designing Win Themes™, I would recommend that sales leaders consider a messaging hierarchy. The top of the pyramid, when it comes to large, strategic accounts, would be Win Themes™. The next level of the pyramid would be value propositions. Value props are comprehensive and have their own components, but key aspects that support account-based Win Themes™ should be integrated into the overall messaging. The next level in the hierarchy are the differentiators. And finally, the elevator pitch can be fine-tuned using Win Themes™ as the basis. During the course of sales conversations, features and benefits should be used during appropriate times such as product demonstrations. Proof, or as Lisa Magnuson calls it "Evidence," will back up the entire pyramid.

When building your hierarchy, alignment is key. All of the levels should be carefully planned and integrated in light of the stream of conversations that make up the entire sales process. I frequently observe account teams rushing to share everything at once. Themes should be doled out over time.

Account teams who understand how all these powerful concepts relate to one another and where each sits within the pyramid are in a position to prevail over their competitors.

Advance Nine: Engaging Executives

"It is not necessary to do extraordinary things to get extraordinary results."

—WARREN BUFFETT

Purpose

- Executives, by nature, are concerned with the long term, and therefore respond well to a long-term cultivation strategy.
- Approach executive engagement in a systematic manner.
- Enjoy the full benefits of access and inclusion associated with carefully cultivated executive relationships.
- For large opportunities, lack of an executive sponsor can cost you the loss of the contract.

Executive Engagement Overview

The goal of executive engagement is to break the once-and-done cycle that many account teams fall into. Executive cultivation is the process of planning the who, what, when, and how associated with developing and maintaining relationships with senior leaders. Why is it important? The value of key executive relationships is far-reaching. Sure, sometimes top executives are the ultimate decision makers for your products and services. However, many times they simply ratify decisions made by managers or stakeholders. In all cases, executives have a vision for where the company is headed. They set goals and priorities that infiltrate throughout the organization. They can open doors, clear roadblocks and provide access to important resources. In short, they make things happen.

Executive Cultivation Steps

1. Pinpoint your target executive sponsor(s).
2. Conduct extensive research.
3. Engage the account selling team.

4   Create an executive dossier.
5   Determine why the executive would see value in you and your organization.
6   Consider timing from executive's perspective.
7   Refresh research and account strategy work prior to all interactions.
8   Consider the best methods to secure an appointment.
9   Pull out all the stops (pre-call planning) for meeting preparation.
10 Determine the best 'touch points' over the next year and mark your calendar.
11 360º follow up after meetings (Executive, assistant, referrer, sponsor, etc.)

Executive Access – Best Practices

- Seek sponsorship (your internal champion) from within their organization.
- Find referral(s) from outside their organization.
- Develop an account-specific strategy to access key executives. (See Executive Touch Point Suggestions)
- Use your account team and be creative.
- Be patient – it can take a long time to access an executive.

Executive 'Touch Point' Suggestions

- Executive-to-executive connection program (offered by your company)
- Existing customers: annual executive strategic planning meeting
- Ideas for process improvements/cost savings
- Solutions that contribute to the achievement of their goals
- Executive summaries and dashboards (annual executive summary)
- New marketing ideas (for them)
- Information that demonstrates an understanding of their goals/issues
- Articles about trends in their industry
- Articles about trends in their customers' industry
- Competitive intelligence
- Ideas to impact revenue, profit, market share, customer satisfaction or employee satisfaction

- Introductions to other executives
- Executive-appropriate events
- LinkedIn®

Benefits of Executive Engagement

- Consistent access to the key people of influence
- Open lines of communications about important initiatives, programs or changes
- Executive can easily and quickly remove obstacles

Sample Executive Engagement Plan

- Set up alerts for your account to stay informed of important news
- Set up calendar prompts for executive touchpoints
- Augment core meetings with soft touches, such as articles of interest, personal notes, email requests for advice or guidance

Executive Contact	Quarter One	Quarter Two	Quarter Three	Quarter Four
Thomas J. Edwards, CEO SAS Financial	Annual planning meeting	Resource introduction	Annual golf outing	Executive briefing

Executive Briefing Communication

An executive briefing communication, used with current customers, is a powerful, proactive sales tool that communicates the outcomes and impact associated with your solutions to busy executives. The communication format may be a letter, dashboard, email or executive summary. The communication is best delivered in person. Opportunities to discuss your executive briefing communication may be a year-end review or annual planning session. The benefits include:

- Raising the level of awareness of past successes
- Paving the way for executive sponsorship and access in the future
- Providing recognition, as appropriate, for your day-to-day contacts
- Articulating alignment points between your organizations
- Documenting key accomplishments which can be referenced in the future

- Differentiating your company
- Seeding ideas for future initiatives or projects

Executive Dossier Overview

- Company summary
- Executive's background: Job history, professional associations, boards, publications
- Executive photo
- Executive's focus areas or priorities
- Areas of interest/likes or dislikes
- Personal style
- Commonality with your company: alignment areas
- History with your company: current or past relationships
- Key influencers (Inside or outside of the company)
- Contacts in common (Inside or outside of the company)
- Executive assistant

Example Dossier/Brief Sample

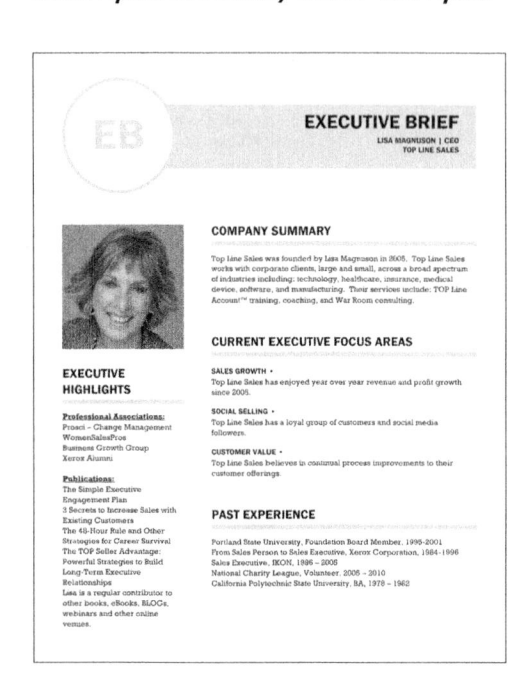

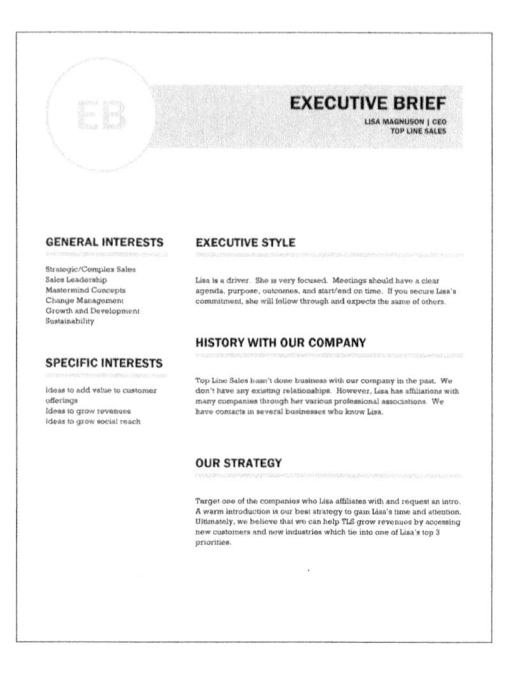

| Name: _____ |
| Company: _____ |

Company Summary

Executive's Background

**Executive's Focus Areas
or Priorities**

Areas of Interest

**Personal style and
communication
preferences**

Alignment Areas

History

Key Influencers

Contacts in Common

Executive Assistant

Top reasons why your executive sponsor would find value in meeting with you:

_____

_____

_____

Advance Ten: Finding Expansion Opportunities

"A goal should scare you a little and excite you a lot."

–JOE VITALE

Purpose

- Assess the account from a holistic perspective to uncover more business opportunities (current or future).
- Align the value that the customer is seeking to the value that your company provides.
- Project or estimate (forecast) all the opportunities, especially long term, for your products and services.
- Understand and map the competitive landscape.
- Avoid scenarios where you find out that your prospect or customer has just purchased a product or service you offer and didn't include you in their buying process.
- Involve the full account team in new business opportunities.

Overview

The goal of the Finding Expansion Opportunities advance is for the sales team to be able to clearly see where they are, where they would like to be and where the competitors currently reside within the customer's environment. Ultimately, the exercise uncovers the potential value alignment between your company and the customer's company.

Finding Expansion Opportunities – Steps

1. **What is your customer trying to achieve?** (I.e. increased profitability, revenue growth, new customers, reduced expenses, process improvements, etc.) Explore how your solutions can impact the areas your customer cares about most.

2. **Analyze the full picture** to see the account's complete opportunity, both short term and long term. The snapshot gives you a value alignment grid from your point of view and the account's point of view.

3. **What areas of your customer's business can you impact?** Think broadly about other departments, other locations, subsidiaries, etc. Would the impact of your solution be high, medium or low relative to what your customer is trying to achieve?

4. **Consider all your offerings**: hardware, software, support, services, partner offerings, etc. in the context of how valuable they would be to your customer. How can you help?

5. **Consider how the customer is solving the problem currently.** Is a competitor providing the solution? Is their current approach working? What are they missing? Are there contractual implications to be considered?

6. **Engage your customer in the process.** Ask the customer to verify their priorities, timeline, current approach, gaps, and desired results. Collaborate on the creation of a strategic map/plan for your partnership. Practical ideas to engage your customer include planning sessions, roadmap sessions, business reviews, problem-solving workshops or visioning summits.

7. **Define the timeline for those opportunities that offer high value**. Is the opportunity available within the short term, midterm or long term?

8. **Act now.** The account-based selling team should discuss what can be done now to prepare for future opportunities.

9. **Develop an action plan.**

Advance Eleven: Tracking Progress

"The way to get started is to quit talking and begin doing."

—WALT DISNEY

Purpose

- Clarity around each action item--who, what, when
- Commitment to move the account forward
- Collaboration through account team discussion and agreement
- Clear documentation of tactics leading to accountability

Action Items

- Review at the beginning of each account war room session
- Summarize, clarify and gain commitment at the end of each account war room session

Tactics Tracking Sample Format

Action Item	Person Responsible	Targeted Completion Date	Actual Completion Date	Comments

PLAY #7

Ramp Up Your Sales Process for Complex Opportunities

"The overarching sales enablement goal from a change management perspective is to shift behavior from everyone doing their own thing to everyone doing the best thing."

–DANIEL ZAMUDIO, FOUNDER & CEO, PLAYBOOX

Play Attributes

The most successful sales organizations follow a sales process based on best practices unique to their customers, organization and industry. Usually that sales process is embedded in the Customer Relationship Management platform. The complex opportunity sales process is commonly an overlay to the existing sales process, not separate. It only differs in depth and breadth. It integrates the activities and tools required to land really large, complex contracts, such as those 5X your average contract size. The purpose of this play is to differentiate between a standard sales process and a 5X sales process and to ramp up to a 5x sales process for all truly large and complex opportunities.

Constructing the Play

Modern sales leadership teams are challenged with lack of visibility into the sales process, consistency of sellers executing on the sales process, sales stage management and overall close ratios. Therefore, clarity around the sales process for complex opportunities is a top priority. Below is a partial list of the benefits of integrating the complex opportunity sales process with your normal sales process. Scenarios that might benefit from separating the complex opportunity sales process from the base line sales process are distinct global or national account programs or companies with unique characteristics to their large opportunity approach.

Account Team Benefits associated with Ramping Up Your Complex Opportunity Sales Process:

- Predictable sales results for big opportunities because account teams depend on a system that codifies the unique attributes of a 5X deal.
- Visibility into what the customer is doing, thinking and feeling during each stage allows the account team to maintain a customer first perspective.
- Clarity on next steps to progress the account team's sales efforts is helpful during pre-call planning and keeps the account team focused over long periods of time.
- A list of value-added resources by stage means account teams can tap into the best and brightest people to move their account strategy forward.
- A handy reference for sales tools at the correct stage promotes account team creativity.
- Following a successful template improves close ratios of longer, complex sales cycles.
- Training the account team on the complex opportunity aspects of the sales process is an excellent way to onboard new account team members and will also enhance team building.

A note about technology enablement. We have intentionally omitted specific mention or evaluation of technology platforms, applications or tools in this Playbook. However, when it comes to the elements needed during each stage to identify, develop and close really big, complex deals, the most successful and productive sales organization use sophisticated technology platforms to enable account teams. Technology platforms that are most helpful for account teams include:

- Access from anywhere and via any device.
- Visual design interface that is conducive for collaboration among account teams with 5 or more members across vast geographies. For example, a compelling user experience that's easy to use for:
  - Gathering account insights
  - Relationship mapping (think org chart design versus list of contacts)
  - Strategy charting (think pre-strategy SWOT, short, medium and long-term account goals)
  - Win Theme™ development
  - Competitive analysis and blocking
  - Tactics tracking
  - Communicating important updates to all account team members
- Access by all account team members*

*An important red flag as it relates to technology is to choose a collaboration platform that's accessible to everyone on the account team. If extended members of the account team don't have a seat or license for the collaboration platform, then they will be excluded from team collaboration and critical communications.

Deploying the Play

1. Sales leaders and their teams should evaluate their current sales process and determine what gaps exist in comparison to their *Big Deal* sales process.
2. Sales leaders need to map the stages and associated attributes of their big, complex sales opportunities to capture the unique characteristics of the 5X sales process.
3. Sales leaders should decide if their complex opportunity sales process should be separate and distinct or integrated.
4. The *Big Deal* sales process can then either be integrated into the standard sales process or established as a distinct sales process. In either case, account teams can navigate the increasingly complex B2B buying process, which includes more people involved in the decision process and more due diligence on the part of buyers.

5. Key performance indicators should be developed for the *Big Deal* sales process. The indicators will be very different from a standard sales process. For example, the time it takes to work through each stage will most likely be dramatically different for 5X deals.

6. The *Big Deal* sales process should be managed by sales leadership with a similar frequency to the standard sales process during forecasting, deal coaching, territory planning, business reviews and during sales manager field travel days.

7. In addition to daily use of the process, the *Big Deal* sales process should be used by account teams during pre-call planning and account strategy meetings (war room meetings). For example, account teams can check the unique characteristics of the stage, resources that might be helpful to the account team or sample questions which can be used for pre-call planning.

Yellow and Red Flag Alerts

Examples of Yellow Flags

- Account teams struggle to identify which stage of the sales process they're in.
- Account teams aren't clear on the extra work needed inside of each stage for complex opportunities.
- Account teams aren't aware of or don't use all the tools and resources available to them.
- Sales leaders and managers lack a system to reinforce and recognize progress.

Examples of Red Flags

- Big deals are stalled or don't close due to lack of compliance to the process.

Defensive Remedies

- Follow all Sales Leader Playbook best practices.
- Conduct in depth account team training on the complex opportunity sales process highlighting the unique characteristics of the complex opportunity sales process versus the baseline sales process.

- Develop key performance indicators to evaluate the health and forward movement of the big deal sales process. Indicators should include leading indicators (advance notice) as well as lagging indicators (review of the past).
- Use the stage specific coaching questions to help account teams move forward.

Playbacks

Check out the related Play #4 Mentor and Develop Account Teams, specifically the Coaching Questions by Stage.

Check out the related Play #6 Commit to a Strategic Opportunity Model.

Check out the related Play #9 Designate and Enable Account Quarterbacks.

Check out the related Play #12 Conduct Internal 5X Business Reviews.

Play Models

THE TOP LINE ACCOUNT™ SALES PROCESS SAMPLE

DEFINITION OF STAGE	CHARACTERISTICS OF STAGE	CUSTOMER'S PERSPECTIVE
	• X • X • X	• Doing: • Thinking: • Feeling:

Sales Actions

1. X
2. X
3. X
4. X
5. X

Sales Questions Inventory

Criteria To Move To The Next Stage	Sales Tools
• X • X • X	1 X 2 X 3 X
Resources	
• X • X • X	

Here are examples of some **Unique Activities** for a complex opportunity sales process. This list is not meant to be inclusive, only to give you ideas for activities your account teams could perform at each stage of your own process.

Stage: Interest

- Pull together the account-based selling team
- Conduct deep research
- Gather account insights
- Hold pre-call planning with the account team for prospect meetings

Stage: Qualify

- Score the account
- Schedule a war room account strategy session
- Determine tools and resource people who can help
- Refine account research and insights
- Identify the executive sponsor and key stakeholders
- Hold pre-call planning with the account team for prospect meetings

Stage: Develop

- Engage the account team in the development of the Strategy Brief (i.e., Relationship Map, Pre-Strategy SWOT, Strategy Chart, Win Theme™ development, Competitive Analysis)
- Use strategy tools such as the RFP/Big Deal Success Calculator™
- Engage the executive sponsor
- Schedule more war room account strategy sessions
- Hold pre-call planning with the account team for prospect meetings

Stage: Propose

- Continue work on the Strategy Brief (i.e., Relationship Map, Pre-Strategy SWOT, Strategy Chart, Win Theme™ development, Competitive Analysis)
- Schedule more war room account strategy sessions
- Hold pre-call planning with the team for presentations, proposals or demos (Use Win Themes™)

Stage: Conclude

- Continue work on the Strategy Brief (i.e., Relationship Map, Pre-Strategy SWOT, Strategy Chart, Win Theme™ development, Competitive Analysis)
- Schedule more war room account strategy sessions
- Hold pre-call planning with the team for prospect meetings
- Conduct win retrospective with new customer
- Celebrate with the entire account team

Stage: Expand

- Develop executive engagement roadmap
- Update research and insights
- Create proactive account management approach
- Use the Expanding Expansion Opportunities Advance to create a plan
- Refresh the Strategy Brief (i.e., Relationship Map, Pre-Strategy SWOT, Strategy Chart, Win Theme™ development, Competitive Analysis)
- Hold Pre-call planning with the team prior to important customer meetings

Sideline Coach: Expert Opinion
Daniel Zamudio, Founder & CEO, Playboox

When it comes to ramping up your sales process for complex opportunities, there are three legs to the stool that must be considered: a sales process that forces a strategic approach, best practices unique to complex opportunities and technology to support the entire process.

Technology Leg. A few thoughts from the perspective of a technology company founder:

- In order to scale or ramp, technology is a must.
- Solve the business problem first, then apply the correct technology.
- In the spirit of crawl, walk, run, just because it's a complex opportunity sales process, applying technology doesn't have to be a big deal.
- Start small. For example, start with relationship mapping.
- Companies can build first, then build to last.
- Choose a technology framework that's flexible and agile.
- Professional enterprise salespeople require professional technology-enabled tools.
- The best technology tools teach salespeople to be more strategic by following the process.

Complex Sales Process Leg. Another view on ramping up your sales process for complex opportunities is to consider the problem from another angle. Instead of thinking about complex opportunities as a sales effort, what if complex opportunities were considered a *project* necessitating a project management approach? What skill sets, mind sets and tool sets would then be required? There are many parallels and possibly some perspective breakthroughs for account teams, specifically the account quarterback. For example:

- **Skill Sets:** Does the account quarterback run a complex sales process with the precision of an experienced project manager? Are they allocating resources, managing timelines and developing contingency plans? This mindset shift might be extremely helpful and result in the account team's understanding why following a structured approach leads to improved results. Customers will also recognize this level of professionalism.
- **Mind Sets:** The complex opportunity sales process is similar to your regular sales process; the difference is simply a matter of depth. It's like the difference between

an easy project and a big, complex project. The framework is the same, but the depth is dramatically different. For example, research is a key component of every sales process, but the depth of the research and the time spent on research for a complex opportunity are drastically different.

- **Tool Sets:** Professional people need professional tools. Would a large project team try to manage all the complexities of a multi-year project without solid tools? Of course not. Account teams going after extremely large contracts require tools sets that are technology-enabled.

Best Practices Leg. When I think of best practice levers for Sales VPs, I'm mindful of their two most important priorities: keeping and growing existing large customers and closing new big account deals. To that end, I'd like to share a few of my favorite mantras and quotes:

"Best practice as it relates to ramping up your sales process for complex opportunities means capturing, codifying and institutionalizing the behaviors of the best account teams. The result is that all account teams will have immediate access to what top performing teams say, ask, do and use at each stage of the sales process."

–Dan Zamudio mantra

"If you want to teach people a new way of thinking, don't bother trying to teach them. Instead, give them a tool, the use of which will lead to new ways of thinking."

– Buckminster Fuller, American author, inventor & systems theorist

"A complex sales process does not need to be complex."

–Dan Zamudio mantra

"Even experts need checklists – written guides that walk them through the key steps in any complex procedure."

–Atul Gawande, Surgeon & author Checklist Manifesto

PLAY #8

Develop Competitive Blocking Strategies

"Expect the best. Prepare for the worst. Capitalize on what comes."

–ZIG ZIGLAR

Play Attributes

The purpose of engaging in competitive analysis is for the sales account team to analyze their position relative to the competition in order to prepare for a successful outcome. Most 5X deals include heavy competition. The account team's competitive focus includes analyzing each competitor, developing counter measures including setting landmines and establishing tactics to overcome the competition to win the business.

Constructing the Play

- Analyzing the competition early and often enables the selling team to stay one step ahead.

- A 360° view of your competitors offers the best perspective. The customer's view, your competitor's view of themselves and your assessment (view) and analysis based on research and competitive intelligence.
- Competitive blocks (blocking your competitors' advances), either proactive or reactive, are very powerful in competitive situations. It's also important for the account team to consider competitive trends and how they may or may not affect your strategy and goals. Competitive trends may include:
    - Prospects learn about your company and its products and services well before they contact you.
    - Prospects come to the table educated on the competitive playing field (their options to solve their problem.)
    - Competitors continue to improve and change.
    - More people involved in the decision process can lead to increased options to solve problems.
    - Non-traditional competitors can emerge.

Deploying the Play

1. Ask the account team to gather competitive intelligence (CI). The straightforward approach below will help the account team cover all the basics.

Competitive Intel	Competitor Type (Formidable, Average, Minor)
About/General	
Direction/Strategies for Growth	
Their Differentiators	
Target Market(s)/Top Customers	
Products/Services/Capabilities	
People	
Known Relationships with Customer/Prospect	
Pricing/Costs/Value	
Distribution Channels/Sales Model	

Competitive Intel	Competitor Type (Formidable, Average, Minor)
Reputation	
Changes/News	
Other	

2. Help the account team to do a competitive SWOT analysis from the competitor's perspective. Ask these questions as if you were in the fox hole as the competitor.

   a. Where do we have the advantage?
   b. Where does the competition have an advantage?
   c. How can we leverage our advantage?
   d. How can we neutralize their advantage?
   e. What do we need to do to win?
   f. What will they do to win?
   g. Do we have actions to capitalize on our advantages?
   h. Do we have actions to address our disadvantages?

3. Work with the account team to create a prospect criteria analysis.

Prospect Buying Criteria(Explicit Needs) *	Your Company**	Competitor A**	Competitor B**

*
S=Stated Criteria
U=Unstated Criteria

**
A=Advantage
D=Disadvantage
N=Neutral
U=Unknown

Prospect Criteria Analysis Notes

- List buying criteria (explicit needs) in order of importance to the prospect or customer.
- Label each criterion as 'stated' or 'unstated' by the prospect or customer.
- Discuss advantages, disadvantages, neutral and unknowns for your company as well as each competitor.
- Analyze learnings from all information gathered.
- Determine actions.

At last the account team is in a safe position to develop competitive blocks. In order to develop both proactive and re-active competitive blocks, the account team should:

- Think through pre-emptive strike opportunities. (Proactive)
- Consider tactics to seed landmines for competitors. (Proactive)
- Develop tactics to block competitors' strikes. (Reactive)
- Anticipate key competitor's actions. (Proactive)
- Think through your competitor's response to your blocks. (Proactive)

Proactive Competitive Block Examples

- Install a pilot program to garner internal support before a competitor.
- Get in early to help shape buying criteria to align with your products and services.
- Initiate an account-based target marketing plan.
- Capitalize on focused prospect programs such as special events or webinars.
- Use an assessment tool to diagnose, assess or analyze a critical area early in the sales process.
- Partner with a competitor to block a more formidable competitor.

Reactive competitive block examples

- Tap into your internal champion for intelligence on competitive activity and adjust accordingly.
- Ask your executive sponsor to intervene on your behalf if a competitor is putting you in a bad position.
- Acquire a problematic competitor.

- Try to influence the prospect to change their criteria midstream.
- Change the game with new information.

4   Lead a collaboration with the account team to develop competitive blocks.

Proactive	Reactive

Yellow and Red Flag Alerts

Examples of Yellow Flags

- Prospect criteria has changed to the advantage of your competitor.

Examples of Red Flags

- Prospect has gone silent.

Defensive Remedies

- Follow the best practices outlined in this Playbook.
- Gather the account team for 'Plan B' which usually includes reactive competitive blocks.

Play Models

COMPETITIVE STRATEGY CHECKLIST

TOP Line Account™ Competitive Strategy Checklist

- ☐ Get in early to help shape the customer's buying criteria. (explicit needs)
- ☐ Seek out questions, concerns and objections early and address completely so they don't come up later in the sales cycle.
- ☐ Identify customer snipers or threats.
- ☐ Use your resources: competitive intelligence, employees who worked for competitors, past experience with competitor.
- ☐ Uncover your competitors' landmines.
- ☐ Focus most of your time on your prospect's problems and opportunities. (Versus focusing on your competition)
- ☐ Best to convey your strengths versus attacking the competitor's weaknesses.
- ☐ Rise above the competition with your knowledge of the prospect's business and industry and your knowledge of your company's resources, products and services.
- ☐ Design a strategy and solution that locks out the competition.
- ☐ Understand what will make your decision-maker successful.
- ☐ Pay close attention to changing and evolving decision criteria.
- ☐ Put yourself in your competitors' shoes to anticipate their moves.
- ☐ Ask yourself, 'Who is my competitor talking to?' (Find their internal champions and executive sponsors.)
- ☐ Add new information on a regular basis to competitive archives and share with account team members.
- ☐ Don't take your eye off the competition until your contract is signed.

Playbacks

Check out the related Play #11 Mobilize War Rooms.

Sideline Coach: Expert Opinion
Christopher Ryan, CEO, Fusion Marketing Partners, Author of *B2B Revenue Playbook* and *Winning B2B Marketing*

I would like to share 13 competitive blocking strategies. While these strategies can be applied at the macro or company level, I've tailored them to the account team level. Competitors are serious business, and thoroughly understanding and disrupting them, either proactively or reactively, is necessary to win more often.

1. **Go outside to complete your competitor SWOT.** Conducting competitor SWOT analysis is a very effective way to uncover your own vulnerabilities. To really get to the truth, however, turn to your customers, partners and stakeholders. Ask them two questions:

    a   How can competitors beat us?

    b   How can we beat them?

    Once you learn the truth, address weaknesses by shoring up, filling gaps and reinforcing your strengths.

2. **Pivot.** If the account team can't figure out a way to block your competitors, pivot to a place where you have more control over the outcome. That way you can play the game on your battleground, not theirs.

3. **Get out ahead.** Figure out which competitors can disrupt your plan and get there first. An example might be a well-timed and well-placed assessment.

4. **Decide to come in late.** Sometimes the best strategy is to sit on the sidelines and wait until the conditions are favorable and then spring into action. For example, a prospect may be doing a lot of shopping, comparing and analyzing. Let them get downstream in their buying process and then enter when there's clarity and commitment.

5. **Build relationships before there's a deal on the table.** Get to know potential prospects before they are shopping. Build trust. Follow key contacts on social media and comment on their postings. People like people who think they are smart. Be genuine but use time to your advantage in building key relationships. Encourage your account team to engage executive sponsors thoughtfully and methodically.

6 **Own or control an important part of the supply chain.** This could also apply to your solution. For instance, if you own the analysis phase through the implementation project management phase, you can effectively lock out some competitors.

7 **Use your market leader advantage.** If your company has the largest awareness in the market, then use the safe decision or resource-rich angle.

8 **Use your small size advantage.** If you're not the biggest or well known in the market, then tout flexibility, speed and responsiveness.

9 **Channel partners offer a wealth of information.** Channel partners may have worked with one or more of your competitors at some point. Don't keep them at arm's length. Ask them all about your competitors at a deep level.

10 **Bundle unlikely products or services.** Figure out where your competitors have gaps in their product or services lines and create packages of services or products to block them. For example, you can package training, project management or access to experts as part of your solution.

11 **Consider acquiring**. At the company level, buy another company to complement your offerings. At the account team level, think like an entrepreneur by utilizing partners to fill missing pieces or gaps.

12 **Refuse to play the pricing game.** Studies show that holding prices firm increases overall revenue. It also can add value to your solution and certainly bolsters your credibility. However, pricing is always within the context of your offering and where it falls on the high value to commodity spectrum. Play the long game with pricing and hold steady when you can.

13 **Simplicity is a big differentiator.** If your competitor's process makes it difficult for customers to buy from them, use their complexity to your advantage. Talk about (and demonstrate) the benefits of your simple and efficient buying processes.

PART THREE

Sales Execution Plays

---

*"Ability is what you're capable of doing.
Motivation determines what you do.
Attitude determines how well you do it."*

–LOU HOLTZ

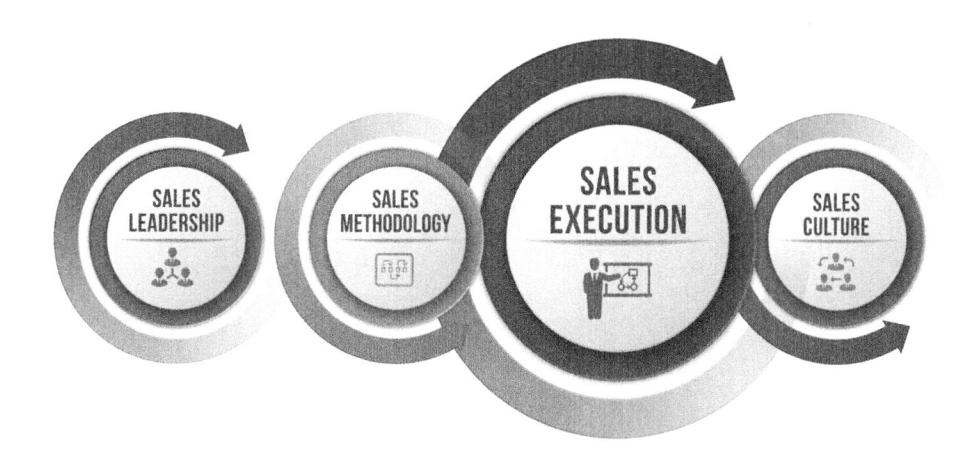

In this Part

5X Deal Sales Execution Includes…

- Designating and enabling account quarterbacks
- Installing pre-call planning acumen
- Mobilizing war rooms
- Conducting internal 5X business reviews (IBRs)

Sales Leader Interview Findings

Top Line Sales, January 2019

I completed over 40 hours of live interviews with 41 Sales VP between February and October 2018. Among my findings: **Playbooks--Not Just for Sales Reps**

97% of sales leaders believe that a sales leader playbook would be extremely valuable and positively affect their priorities while helping to address their challenges.

Only 14% of respondents have a formal sales *leader* playbook.

The majority of sales leaders interviewed indicated they have a sales playbook for their sellers.

Part Three: Sales Execution Plays specifically addresses the need for sales leaders to have executable tactics at their disposal, much as they provide these for their sellers.

Take your team to the next level by creating your custom **Sales Leader Playbook**:

Downloadable templates make it easy for your sales leadership team to build your own unique approach to leadership, methodology, execution and culture for a 5X deal generating sales organization. No need to start from scratch. Customizable templates available at *www.toplinesales.com*.

PLAY #9

Designate and Enable Account Quarterbacks

"Success is the sum of small efforts, repeated day-in and day-out."

–ROBERT COLLIER

Play Attributes

The account quarterback is a critical role for all account teams. The purpose of this play is for sales leaders to understand that account quarterbacks must be formally designated and continually enabled. Whether the opportunity for a 5X contract is an existing customer expansion or a new prospect (new logo), the quarterback is the hub around which all account activity rotates. For this reason, the sales leader needs to both sanction this role and enable it over time.

Constructing the Play

The earmarks of an outstanding account quarterback include:
- Belief that truly big deals are won as a team

- Ability to facilitate, lead and direct
- Strong resource coordination
- Comprehensive communication skills
- Tactical and strategic thinking abilities
- Focus on the customer or prospect and the ability to help the team put themselves in the customer's shoes
- Attention to detail and organized
- Strength to maintain account team discipline to the methodology
- Commitment to provide ongoing account team recognition and encouragement
- Unwavering belief and commitment to account development and closure over the long haul

Deploying the Play

1. Designate the account quarterback. Review that role as it relates to the account team. Set expectation with AE/AM that they will be expected to be the account quarterback, with your strong support and back up. Discuss how best to support and enable them in their role.

2. Build up the AE/AM to take the reins as account quarterback. For example, shift control gradually over time.

3. Know the methodology and make sure the account lead knows the methodology. Have a clear understanding of where you are in the TOP Line Account™ development process and where you're going.

4. Act as back up facilitator during the war rooms until the AE/AM is ready to take the helm.

5. Demonstrate strong facilitation skills during war room account strategy sessions in these ways:

    a. Make sure everyone is engaged and giving their best.
    b. Start and end on time.
    c. Time – stay on track – assign a timekeeper but monitor yourself as well.
    d. Set meeting ground rules for dysfunctional groups.

- e Assign a reliable note taker. Check in with them during the meeting to make sure they're capturing everything including due dates. Ask them to review all action items at the end of the war room.
- f Strong tone of voice--command the group.
- g Call out dysfunctional behavior in a professional manner.
- h Keep energy level high during the meeting; build enthusiasm and excitement to achieve account goals.
- i Encourage the account team to constantly assess resources--who else can add value to the account and/or team?

6 Sales leaders should volunteer for top level action items only. For example, executive related activities.

7 Make sure AE/AM sends out an agenda in advance. End each meeting with a review of action items and input on the agenda for the next meeting.

8 Recognize team for all accomplishments, both big and small.

9 Coach account quarterback on how to maintain momentum and accountability. For example,
- a Get notes and next meeting invite sent out within 48 hours after each war room session.
- b Include agenda in meeting invite and share via email.
- c Consider all the people who should be included. Keep stakeholders and account resources up to date by including them as an FYI.
- d Update account team on important progress through emails to entire account team. This practice maintains momentum and keeps mind share high for the opportunity.
- e Complete all your action items promptly and share results.
- f Check-ins: check in with team members who have important tasks or people who have a history of not completing action items.

10 Avoid the following pitfalls:
- a Frequent re-scheduling of war room strategy meetings, which results in loss of momentum and accountability.
- b Start late, end late, which is disrespectful of people's time.

- c Stay true to the agenda and avoid getting sidetracked. If the strategy meetings aren't productive, value-added resources will stop attending.
- d Create a "parking lot" for issues that can be better solved later.
- e Use strong facilitation skills to ensure every attendee is engaged. Don't let one person, even a senior executive, dominate the meeting.
- f Recognize the team for all accomplishments!

11 Mentor account quarterback about how to add value and demonstrate leadership during war room strategy meetings. Examples include:

- a Offer at least one or two breakthrough ideas during account strategy war room meetings.

    For example, account quarterback explains what's important to the customer's customer and asks, How does our solution help them?

- b Ask general questions to prompt strategic thinking from group:
    - i Does anyone have any ideas on …?
    - ii We have one idea to move us forward, let's consider other options before we decide.
    - iii Let's brainstorm solutions to solve …
    - iv Stepping back from our current thought process, what are we missing?

- c Ask prospect focused questions to pull strategic thinking from group:
    - i How long has this problem been going on?
    - ii What areas of the organization/people are impacted by this problem?
    - iii How does the organization measure the impact of problems?
    - iv Have they tried to solve this problem in the past? If so, what happened?
    - v What will happen if the problem isn't solved? (Impact to revenue, expenses, customer satisfaction) How do they measure?
    - vi Who's involved in trying to solve the problem?
    - vii Who will make the final decision to move forward or not?
    - viii What are their criteria?
    - ix Could the solution help or apply to other parts of the organization?
    - x How could the solution be expanded?

    d Keep track of good ideas from other account strategy sessions and offer them up to the group.

    e Challenge the group's thinking. Push back; force new ideas and alternatives.

    f Ask the team to consider possible roadblocks. Use questions to promote broad thinking:

        i   Is anyone blocking the initiative?

        ii   Are there any critical events, time frames or roadblocks driving the situation?

        iii Are there any other issues surrounding this opportunity we need to consider?

        iv Who will likely be the competition for this business opportunity? Who are their contacts?

    g Recognize team for all accomplishments--big and small.

    h Celebrate successes.

    i   Promote account team learning.

Yellow and Red Flag Alerts

Examples of Yellow Flags

- Account quarterback taking the reins slowly.
- Account quarterback lacking in a key area such as team communication or using resources wisely.
- Lack of team clarity on who is the account quarterback, i.e., is it the Sales VP or AE/AM?

Examples of Red Flags

- Account quarterback selling as a lone wolf.
- Dysfunctional account team behaviors.

Defensive Remedies

- Follow the best practices outlined in this Playbook.
- Intensify coaching with account quarterback.
- As a last resort, designate another team member as account quarterback.

Playbacks

Check out the related Play #1 Inspire and Activate Account Teams.

Check out the related Play #2 Establish 5X Deal Sales Expectations.

Check out the related Play #4 Mentor and Develop Account Teams.

Check out the related Play #11 Mobilize War Rooms.

Play Models

See 'TOP Line Account™ Seller Expectations' in Part One.

See 'Team and Resources' in Part Two/Advance #3.

See 'Agreeing on Team Guidelines' in Part Two/Advance #4

Sideline Coach: Expert Opinion
**Bob Apollo, Founder, Inflexion-Point Strategy Partners –
B2B Value-based Selling Experts**

The account quarterback must believe that every member of the account team is capable of adding value, and account team meetings must reflect this with every member of the team encouraged to 'speak the truth' regarding any aspects of the account team's work.

Aggressive bulldozer behavior on the part of the account quarterback, particularly anything that has the effect of suppressing candid feedback, is dysfunctional and ultimately unproductive. Just as in an operating theatre even the most junior nurse or assistant must have the power to speak up if they see something that could compromise the operation, so any account team member must feel they are able to bring up something that they believe might compromise the mission.

Inclusion can be encouraged through effective meeting management. Seeking out everyone's views rather than relying on a few vocal contributors can help to ensure that nothing important gets ignored or missed.

With the support and encouragement of the quarterback, the account team must embrace a customer-centric focus. We need to recognize that significant buying decisions are inherently complicated, often non-linear and frequently involve large numbers of involved stakeholders.

The account team needs to acknowledge that in a world where our customers have many potential projects and finite resources, our competition is not restricted to other similar vendors. The project on which we are working is also typically competing against all the other ways in which our customer could choose to invest their scarce resources.

Our customers will always have more potential projects than they have the bandwidth to deal with. The account quarterback must encourage the team to view the world from the customer's perspective, and to consider issues such as:

- What is causing the customer to start searching for new solutions?
- Why is it important for the customer or prospect to take action?
- What is the relative priority of your project to all the other projects that the prospect is tackling?
- Does the account team (and the prospect) fully understand the problem value gap–in other words, the relative size of the problem compared to the effort to solve the problem or the value that will be gained by solving the problem?

The account team needs to get a clear sense of the size of the problem value gap -- the difference between the customer's current situation and their desired future state. Whenever this gap is relatively small, the account team needs to look for ways of selling the need for change by helping the customer to see their threats as more dangerous, and their opportunities as more attractive, than sticking with the status quo.

If these foundations aren't laid early, there is a real risk of disappointment later in the sales process if the customer puts your project on hold or decides to stay with the status quo.

Your proposal needs to promote the customer's need for change as strongly as it promotes the benefits of adopting your solution. No executive summary is complete without a powerful précis, reviewed and pre-agreed with the customer, that covers:

- The customer's current situation and desired future state
- The catalysts or triggers that have caused them to acknowledge the need for change
- The customer's current challenges and the consequences of failing to address them
- The constraints that might be holding them back and the changes that are now required
- The capabilities that any solution must offer, and the clear contrast between your approach to delivering them and all other options
- A conclusion that gives the customer confidence in your proposal

This story needs to be built and tested progressively throughout the engagement with the account team.

Finally, a key role of the quarterback is to anticipate and eliminate avoidable sources of error in the account management process. This revolves around establishing what we need to know and do to execute a successful strategy and ensuring that the team neither misses vital pieces of information nor fails to complete tasks that we know to be critical.

A checklist approach is absolutely invaluable. This can ensure that the account team collectively and individually follows acknowledged best practices and avoids making unjustified assumptions. Simply completing the identified tasks is not enough; the quarterback must ensure that the actions and outcomes are discussed.

For example, simply going through the motions of creating a stakeholder map isn't enough. The team needs to understand each stakeholders' attitudes, motivations, decision role and relationships with all the other members of the customer's decision team.

The account quarterback's role is not just to call the plays but to assess and if necessary, adjust or refine them. They need to acknowledge that sales is a team sport that requires every member of the team, whether they currently have the ball or not, and whether they are currently on the field or on the bench to make their full contribution throughout the game.

PLAY #10

Install Pre-Call Planning Acumen

"The common denominator of success—the secret of success of every man (or woman) who has ever been successful—lies in the fact that he (or she) formed the habit of doing things that failures don't like to do."

—ALBERT E.N. GRAY: THE COMMON DENOMINATOR OF SUCCESS

Play Attributes

The goal of pre-call planning, used in all stages of the sales process, is to think through all the important aspects of a sales call in advance of the meeting. It starts with a clear understanding of which stage of your sales process you're in and where the prospect is in their buying journey. Advance planning ensures you and all participants are on the same page prior to the customer meeting, thereby increasing the overall effectiveness of the call. Ultimately, consistent pre-call planning improves your ability to manage desired change for the customer effectively in order to optimize your sales results.

Constructing the Play

Sales leaders must know the cost of each customer meeting:

- Real costs
- Opportunity costs

Pre-Call Planning is **NOT**

- Doing quick research before a call
- Simply having an agenda
- Planning for your customer meeting without involving the other meeting participants
- Sketching out a couple of points for the call a few minutes prior to the meeting

Deploying the Play

1. Establish the expectation that pre-call planning is the baseline approach to preparing for sales meetings.
2. For 5X deal calls, gather the account team to plan for critical sales calls.
3. Discuss the sales process stage and what the prospect is doing, thinking and feeling at this stage of their buying process.
4. Share results of pre-work such as insights gained from prospect research.
5. Review meeting attendees and their dispositions. Consider who should attend from the account team.
6. Discuss the goals for the meeting--both your goals and the prospect's goals.
7. Brainstorm the desired next steps that would ideally occur after the meeting. Nail down both best and next best. Note that the most powerful next steps represent a shared commitment from the prospect and your team.
8. Jot down all the key questions you would like to ask. (Reference your stage-appropriate sales process questions.)
9. Design your Win Themes™ and how you plan to weave them into the agenda.
10. Anticipate the things that might go wrong and how you can address them. For example, if you have experience with the prospect and know that the decision

maker rarely attends the meeting, then what can you do? Ideas might include asking that person for input on the agenda, asking them to present something, making sure there's value for them by attending.

11   Craft your agenda taking all the pre-work into consideration.

12   After the meeting, debrief the call with the internal team. What did you learn? Clarity on who is the lead for next steps or action items. What call improvements should be made for the next meeting?

Yellow and Red Flag Alerts

Examples of Yellow Flags

- Lack of clarity on roles for the internal team leading to a less than productive prospect meeting.
- No commitment from the prospect on next steps.
- Prospect seems to lack confidence in you and your company after the meeting.

Examples of Red Flags

- No commitments or forward momentum towards a sale.
- Stalled sales process.
- Prospect perceived meeting as a waste of time.

Defensive Remedies

- Follow the best practices outlined in this Playbook.
- Provide training for sellers on the value and how to do pre-call planning.
- Set expectations to make pre-call planning a habit.
- Only go on sales calls for which a pre-call plan can be reviewed well in advance of the meeting.
- Follow all steps in the Play.

Play Models

PRE-CALL PLANNING WORKSHEET

Pre-Call Planning Worksheet

Account: _____   Meeting Date: _____

Sales Process Stage: _____

Pre-Work

☐ Website Review ☐ Send Agenda in Advance/Ask for Customer Input
☐ CRM or History ☐ LinkedIn®/Social Media

Meeting Attendees

Customer Attendees	Title	Role	Strategic Position	Political Influence

*Role: (DM) decision maker, (DI) decision influencer, (U) unknown
**Strategic Position: (P) promoter, (N) neutral, (T) threat, (U) unknown
***Political Influence: (H) high, (M) medium, (L) low, (U) unknown

Goals of the Meeting

Customer Goals

Your Goals

Desired Next Steps from the Meeting (Best and Next Best)

_____

_____

Key Questions/Win Themes™

_____

_____

Anticipate Issues

What Could Go Wrong During Meeting?	Plan B to Prevent or Address?

Agenda

Time	Topic	Purpose
min		
min		
min		
min		
min		

Post-Call Debrief

Key Learnings:

_____

_____

Call Improvements for Next Time:

_____

_____

Next Steps/Action Items

Action Item	Person Responsible	Targeted Completion Date	Actual Completion Date	Comments

TOP LINE ACCOUNT™ SAMPLE AGENDA

Sample Prospect/Customer Meeting Agenda

Time	Topic	Conversation Leader	Notes
XX min.	Open the meeting: • Build rapport • Introductions (with impact) • State the purpose/goals of meeting/review agenda/anything to add? • Gain commitment for objectives		Introductions should focus on value to the customer, not simply job title
XX min.	Review/Updates: • Review of prior meetings/conversations • Ask about new information/updates from their organization • Share what you learned from pre-work • Share facts, statistics to disrupt the status quo and motivate them to think differently about their issues and opportunities		Most productive if the customer has a formal role throughout the agenda

Time	Topic	Conversation Leader	Notes
XX min.	Questions/Listening: • Uncover needs and priorities • Deep dive/ discovery questions • Make observations or suggestions (challenge the status quo) • Seed possible next steps		Use good questions Customer should do the majority of the talking
XX min.	Summarize: • Key points • Problems/Implications/How you can help (Features/benefits/impact) • Opportunities/Implications/ How you can help (Features/benefits/impact) • Points of Differentiation (Win Themes™)		Share evidence, examples, stories of similar customer situations
XX min.	Close Meeting: • Suggest and gain agreement on next steps • Set date of next meeting • Summarize action items		

SUCCESSFUL MEETING CHECKLIST

☐ Have you engaged the account team in formal pre-call planning?

☐ What are the objectives and purpose for the meeting? Does your agenda support attainment of meeting goals?

☐ Have you forwarded the agenda in advance to all participants and asked for input? (Does the customer have a formal role on the agenda?)

- ☐ Have you checked the account team & resources list to make sure the right people have been included?
- ☐ Are meeting logistics clear to all participants? (i.e., day, time, location, attire, technology, meeting format)
- ☐ Have you checked for recent news or updates relevant to the customer prior to the meeting? (and re-checked CRM or relevant account history)
- ☐ Do you know how will you differentiate yourself and your company through this meeting? Are the meeting attendees on your team clear on the Win Themes™ so they can be used throughout the meeting?
- ☐ Do you have information (facts, statistics, insights) prepared to disrupt their thinking about the status quo and thereby help motivate them to want to move forward to solve their problems?
- ☐ Do you know where the company is in their buying cycle? What is your prospect doing, thinking and feeling at the current stage?
- ☐ Do you have thoughtful questions prepared to help move the customer forward?
- ☐ Have you anticipated the issues or objections that may come up during the meeting? Do you have Plan B developed to address?
- ☐ Have you anticipated the next steps that you would like to occur after the meeting?
- ☐ Will you end the meeting by asking attendees if the session was valuable? (I.e., pros and cons or pros and changes for next time.)
- ☐ Are you prepared to follow up with the meeting attendees within 48-hours to keep momentum high?
- ☐ Do you have a "parking lot" for side issues or tangents?
- ☐ Do you have clear assignments for roles to make the meeting run smoothly? (I.e., time keeper, note taker/action items, facilitator)
- ☐ Do you have a reliable system for capturing key information and action items in a format that's sharable with the entire account team?
- ☐ Have you thought about ideas to make the meeting engaging, fun or motivating?
- ☐ Do you have a list of people to thank for their role in making the meeting successful? (I.e. meeting arrangers, referrers, your internal champion)

PRE-CALL PLANNING EFFECTIVENESS ASSESSMENT

Summary

If you're a sales person, manager or business owner looking to increase the effectiveness of your prospect meetings, then The Top Line Sales™ Call Effectiveness Assessment will give you a baseline from which you can grow.

Name: _____

Date: _____

Instructions

Complete this Assessment by answering each of the questions with an answer of Yes, Maybe or No.

Yes: You can confidently answer 'Yes' to this item. You demonstrate this skill or approach on a regular basis (i.e., habit). You are an expert. (Worth 3 points)

Maybe: You would give this item a tentative 'Maybe'. You exhibit this characteristic from time to time but it's not part of your regular or committed approach. (Worth 1 point)

No: Your answer is 'No'. You do not have a comfort level or expertise associated with this approach. (Worth 0 points)

Sales Call Effectiveness Assessment	Rating
Do you start your pre-call planning with a clear understanding of what sales process stage you're in as well as the unique characteristics of that stage?	
Is the meeting planning based on what the prospect is doing, thinking and feeling during this stage of their buying process?	
Do you conduct research resulting in insights and relevant background intelligence prior to prospect meetings?	
Do you check social media or current news for recent updates on the company or meeting attendees?	
Do you assess meeting attendees, their role, disposition relative to your company and political influence as part of your meeting preparation?	
Do you carefully consider and include resources who might add value to your prospect meeting?	
Can you put yourself in your prospect's shoes and articulate their goals for the meeting?	

Sales Call Effectiveness Assessment	Rating
Do you have clear and measurable goals for the conversation?	
Do you adjust your meeting goals to meet your prospect's meeting goals?	
Are next steps considered in advance of the interaction – both best next steps and second best next steps?	
As appropriate to the sales stage, do you develop or review your Win Themes™ prior to the exchange?	
Does each sales meeting include a list of stage related questions that you would like to ask?	
Do you anticipate what might go wrong during the meeting and develop plans to avoid, resolve or mitigate?	
Do you have a successful prospect meeting checklist that you follow?	
Do you have an agenda, including topics, purpose, discussion leader, time allocations for every formal prospect meeting?	
Does your agenda reflect all your pre-call planning work?	
Do you share your agenda with your prospect in advance to gain input?	
For critical meetings such as demos or presentations, do you gather the account team for pre-call planning?	
Do you have a reliable method to take notes and action items and are these summarized at the end of the meeting?	
Do you consider ways to make the prospect meeting memorable, engaging and even fun?	
Do you follow up with the prospect within 48-hours to keep momentum and visibility high?	
Do you have a formal post meeting assessment process, noting what worked well and changes for next time?	

Scoring Results

50 – 66 Points: Give yourself a pat on the back. You have made pre-call planning a habit and you're reaping the rewards.

26 – 49 Points: You have room to improve but take heart that some small adjustments to your current approach will make a big difference in your results.

25 Points or Less: You have the opportunity to dramatically improve your close ratios by committing to improving. Talk with your sales manager or coach to develop a plan that includes observation and input. You can do it and your hard work will be rewarded.

Sideline Coach: Expert Opinion

James Muir, author of *The Perfect Close* and VP of Sales, ShiftWizard

> *"A consistent finding about successful salespeople is that they put effort into planning. Good selling depends on good planning more than any other single factor."*
>
> – NEIL RACKHAM

Neil Rackham is challenging us to be effective, not just efficient. Effectiveness is doing the right things. Efficiency is reducing the time it takes to do something.

When it comes to preparing for sales meetings, I would like to make the following points:

Setting appropriate sales objectives for each opportunity and appropriate call objectives for each individual encounter will lead to an unbroken chain of successful advances that will ultimately lead to closing the sale and getting the order.

If the customer is not taking action, it is not an advance. Knowing the difference between an advance and a continuation can mean the difference between success and failure.

Becoming proficient at setting advances as your primary and secondary objectives for each sales encounter will dramatically increase your sales outcomes.

I would like to share the Three Magic Pre-Call Questions. Salespeople should know the answers to each of these questions before going into any sales encounter. Knowing the answers will result in magnifying your sales effectiveness many times over. The questions are:

1. Why should this customer see me?
2. What do I want the customer to do?
3. How can I provide value during this encounter?

It all comes together in the agenda. A solid agenda ensures that the time invested in the meeting has a valuable return for everyone involved. Your goals are to obtain your ideal advance and deliver your prospect both edification and unexpected value. The best way to achieve this win-win dynamic is to collaborate with your customer on the agenda.

Every sales call is important and warrants comprehensive planning, especially sales calls leading up to closing your highest value contracts.

PLAY #11

Mobilize War Rooms

"Strategies win the war. Tactics win the battles."

−SUN TZU, THE ART OF WAR

Play Attributes

War room strategy sessions are meant for accounts that have scored high on the Opportunity Score Card and therefore warrant the time and attention required to develop and close the TOP Line Account. The purpose of war room work is to:

- Advance account strategy work for your best opportunities
- Maintain account focus and momentum
- Ensure account team accountability to tactics

Constructing the Play

The sales leader ensures that account lead or quarterback, i.e., AE, AM, NAM, GAM:

- Gathers the account team for in-depth strategy planning on a regular and pro-active basis.

- Assigns various members to review the CRM, social media, web site or other sources of information to gain a full understanding and background on the account and share important insights with the full account team.
- Encourages others to provide regular account updates with the team. Proactive communication between war room meetings helps maintain overall focus and accountability for account progress.
- Updates the Strategy Brief document prior to war room meetings.
- Employs account resources effectively, demonstrating depth and breadth to prospect or customer.
- Works with the account manager for existing accounts to uncover opportunities for upselling and cross-selling and includes the account team to help develop and close.
- Includes win celebrations of 5X deals.

Deploying the Play

Strategy Session Agenda (Sample)

- Welcome/review agenda (assign roles: note taker, time, facilitator, etc.)
- Purpose of meeting
- Review tactics from prior meeting
- Strategy Brief work: (Choose subtopics based on time available.) List of subtopics include:
    - Summary of account background (based on highlights gathered from research)
    - Account scoring results
    - Executive summary
    - Discuss team and resources
    - Develop a team agreement
    - Relationship Map
    - Pre-strategy SWOT
    - Strategy Chart
    - Competitive analysis and blocks
    - Executive engagement

- Pre-call planning
- Summarize tactics (review what, who and when)
- Meeting assessment (worked well, improvements for next time)
- Schedule next account strategy (War Room) meeting

Yellow and Red flag Alerts

Examples of Yellow Flags

- Account quarterback doesn't engage the full account team regularly for war room work.
- War room program launched, then day to day priorities take over.
- Disorganized war room agenda, causing less than productive meetings.
- Account quarterback allows short term tactics to overtake long term strategic thinking.
- Tactics or action items aren't captured; therefore, momentum and accountability are lacking.
- Senior company leaders and stakeholders not bought into long term war room approach; rather, focused on 30-day results.
- Management views war room sessions as an opportunity to audit vs. assist.

Examples of Red Flags

- No account progress.
- Account team surprised by the introduction of a competitor.
- Significant changes within account that the account team is unaware of.

Defensive Remedies

- Follow all Playbook best practices.
- Sales leader must stay involved.
- Sales leader maintains expectation that account team follow the 5X deal methodology.

- Sales leader has a deep understanding of the war room approach and its components.
- At least one member of the account team should be designated to challenge the team's thinking. Healthy debate is critical to the war room approach.
- Sales leader socializes the war room approach and benefits with company leaders and stakeholders to gain their sponsorship.
- Sales leaders monitor account team progress and suggest adjustments as needed.
- Sales leaders bolster skills of account lead through mentoring and regular training.
- Introduction of a competitor triggers an immediate account team war room strategy session focused on competitive analysis and blocks.
- Schedule war rooms in advance on a rotating 3-6-month basis.

Play Models

PRE-WAR ROOM CHECKLIST

Account: _____   Date: _____

Estimated Revenue Value: _____

Sales Stage (Interest, Qualify, Develop, Propose, Conclude, Expand):

_____

War Room Activity Options	Purpose	A, B or C Priority for War Room Work
Scoring the opportunity	Decide if opportunity warrants war room work	
Conducting research/ Insights	Get the full picture and develop insights	
Assigning team and resources	Consider all the people who can contribute	

War Room Activity Options	Purpose	A, B or C Priority for War Room Work
Setting account team agreements	Make sure the account team is on the same page	
Mapping relationships	Identify, assess and set account relationship goals	
Constructing a pre-strategy SWOT	Brainstorm the strengths, weaknesses, opportunities and threats	
Charting the strategy	Account team focus	
Developing Win Themes™	Critical for important customer interactions including finalist presentations and prosposals	
Engaging executives	Work to engage an executive sponsor and cultivate that relationship	
Crafting competitive blocks	Assess competitors and develop proactive and reactive blocks	
Pre-call planning	Essential for all important prospect or customer meetings	
RFP planning	Proactive planning, including Win Theme™ development, Pre-RFP Success Calculator, RFP Roadmap	
Prepping for finalist presentation	Proactive planning, including Win Theme™ development and dry runs	

War Room Attendees

_____

_____

_____

WAR ROOM AGENDA SAMPLE

- Welcome/review agenda (assign roles: note taker, time tracker, facilitator, etc.)
- Senior sales leader message
- Purpose of meeting/ground rules/participation expectations
- General account updates/successes
- Review tactics from prior meeting
- Strategy Brief work: (Choose sub-topics based on time available.)
  - Research results/insights gained
  - Account scoring results
  - Executive summary
  - Discuss team and resources
  - Develop team agreements
  - Relationship Map
  - Pre-strategy SWOT
  - Strategy Chart
  - Competitive analysis and blocks
  - Executive engagement
- Pre-call planning
- Summarize tactics (review what, who and when)
- Meeting assessment (worked well, improvements for next time)
- Schedule next account strategy (War Room) meeting

Playbacks

Check out the related Play #15 Celebrate 5X Wins Across Your Organization

Sideline Coach: Expert Opinion

Alice Heiman, Chief Revenue Officer, Alice Heiman, LLC and Co-Founder, TradeShow Makeover™

Account strategy meetings, or war rooms, are essential to close really big deals. I would like to lend my expertise by sharing three scenarios or stories that most account teams will be able to relate to.

Scenario One: *No need to include the account team. "I have all the bases covered."*

The salesperson felt as if there was nothing more to do. He had four solid contacts and all were on board with the proposal. At this point, it was just a waiting game. No need to waste the time of any other internal resources.

The Sales VP encouraged the Account Executive (AE) to pull together the account team. He pointed out that two people can't fight a war, the entire battalion must be involved. Since the contract was valued at more than $300K, the AE reluctantly agreed.

During the war room meeting, it came to light that several members of the account team knew key people in the prospect's organization. The CEO even knew the economic buyer. The war room session ended with action items for the Sales VP and CEO to reach out to their contacts.

The result: the deal moved forward very quickly once all members of the account team lent their expertise and assistance.

Scenario Two: *"I got a guy." We have all the relationships we need.*

The salesperson started the first war room session by announcing that she has a very strong relationship with the decision maker. Her contact let her know that he has the budget and will make the decision.

The account team pushed back a bit. They pointed out that a $500K contract usually involves more than one person. The war room session was spent searching for likely contacts who might be decision influencers or stakeholders. The account team also searched LinkedIn® for connections. They set a short-term goal around getting warm introductions to others involved in the decision process. They also prepped the Account Executive (AE) for her next meeting with her contact. They encouraged the AE to ask about the impact of the decision on the stakeholders and to suggest that they all meet to discuss.

The result: the account team helped the AE to realize that although her contact was solid, he was a single point of failure for such a large deal. In the process of expanding their relationships, one of the account team members uncovered a decision influencer who would have blocked the decision if she wasn't included early. The team was able to avoid this block through mobilizing the war room team.

Scenario Three: *Expansion business with current customer forecasted to close – goes COLD.*

The account team led by the Account Manager (AM) had been meeting for months. They had great relationships in place and everyone seemed to be on board with the proposal to expand services into another division. However, all of a sudden the opportunity went cold. No one was returning calls.

The team put together a war room agenda to debrief the opportunity, even though it was still open. They went back to their research to test their assumptions. By refreshing their account insights, they learned that there was a recent change in leadership. They also figured out that they didn't have an internal coach, someone who would help them move forward. They regrouped and re-engaged but with current information and a solid plan.

The AM changed the nature of his outreach from checking on the status of the proposal to letting them know that he knew about their recent change of leadership. He empathized with the challenges they must be facing. He asked them how he might be of assistance.

The result: he got an immediate response. His contact apologized for the silence and confirmed that yes, the change in leadership had put things on hold. However, this gave the AM time to develop his relationship with his key contact into that of an internal coach. Eventually the project got back on track.

Take Home Advice

1. Don't skip war rooms. Mobilize your account teams.
2. Make sure the right people are in the room. Lots of different perspectives can mean the difference between winning or not.
3. Follow a structured war room agenda. Otherwise, everyone is just talking with no outcomes or accountability to action.
4. Figure out what you know and what you need to know. Don't skip any of the war room elements.
5. Use the power of war rooms to develop all of the relationships needed today to land 5X deals.

PLAY #12

Conduct Internal 5X Business Reviews (IBRs)

"The difference between a successful person and others is not a lack of strength, not a lack of knowledge, but rather a lack of will."

–VINCE LOMBARDI

Play Attributes

The purpose of internal 5X business reviews (IBRs) is to proactively discuss the health of the 5X pipeline, subsequent movement through the complex opportunity sales process and the overall 5X program. IBRs shouldn't be confused with war room meetings. War room meetings focus on the necessary strategy work to move forward an individual account, while IBRs focus on the bigger picture of 5X deal opportunities. IBRs are an opportunity to monitor and make adjustments to the 5X deal sales expectations that were established, that is, to inspect what you expect!

Constructing the Play

The VP of Sales sets the meetings and the tone, customizes the agenda and invites the appropriate participants. The participants vary based on the size of the sales organization and breadth and depth of the top opportunities in progress. The IBR might include sales managers, directors and account quarterbacks. It's common for IBRs to be scheduled quarterly. The duration of the IBR is dependent on the agenda and number of attendees; however, set aside ample time for this foundational meeting. The location can also set the tone. Some organizations prefer to conduct IBRs off-site to avoid distractions and interruptions.

Deploying the Play

Sales VP should set the schedule for IBRs at the beginning of the year.

The agenda might include the following:

- 5X success stories, big idea sharing, special recognition
- Key performance indicators (KPIs), both leading (indicative of items that influence future performance) and lagging (analysis of past performance) indicators, such as:
  - 5X new logo pipeline review
  - Existing customer 5X expansion pipeline review
  - # of accounts scored
  - # of pre-call plan sheets beyond the qualify stage
  - # of executive outreaches
  - # of customer business reviews conducted
  - # of account plans jointly developed with customers
  - # of war rooms held
  - # of Strategy Briefs completed and % completion
  - # of win/loss retrospectives completed
  - # of win celebrations
- 5X program/system health - working/not working
- Customer satisfaction monitor - stop doing/start doing/maintain
- Vertical market penetration (if applicable)

- 5X training reinforcement
- Forecast

A written recap, especially if expectations have been altered, should follow all IBRs.

Yellow and Red flag Alerts

Examples of Yellow Flags

- IBRs held intermittently.
- Sufficient time isn't allocated for IBRs.
- IBRs get off track and don't follow the agenda, i.e., meeting gets derailed.
- IBRs don't strike the proper tone of inspection and accountability for progress and reinforcement of 5X expectations.

Examples of Red Flags

- Lack of an IBR program/no commitment to IBRs.
- The focus is on a tactic level versus strategic level, i.e., program level versus outlook of a specific deal.
- Flawed execution during IBRs by Sales VP.

Defensive Remedies

Follow all Playbook best practices.

Play Models

INTERNAL BUSINESS REVIEW (IBR) SAMPLE AGENDA

- Welcome/review agenda (assign roles: note taker, time, facilitator, etc.)
- Senior sales leader message
- Purpose of review
- 5X account successes & account team recognition
- Review action items from prior IBR
- Key performance indicators review and forecast:
  - 5X new logo pipeline review
  - Existing customer 5X expansion pipeline review
  - # of accounts scored
  - # of pre-call plan sheets beyond the qualify stage
  - # of executive outreaches
  - # of customer business reviews conducted
  - # of customer jointly developed account plans
  - # of war rooms held
  - # of Strategy Brief's completed (and % completion)
  - # of win/loss retrospectives completed
  - # of win celebrations
- Vertical market or focused market penetration (if applicable)
- Customer satisfaction monitor – stop doing/start doing/maintain
- 5X training reinforcement
- 5X program/system health assessment – working/not working
- Summarize tactics (review what, who and when)
- Meeting assessment (worked well, improvements for next time)
- Schedule next IBR

Playbacks

Check out the related Play #2 Establish 5X Deal Sales Expectations.

Check out the related Play #5 Develop a 12-Month Cadence.

Check out the related Play #16 Debrief, Analyze and Define Best Practices.

Sideline Coach: Expert Opinion
George Bontén, Founder & CEO, Membrain

Sales VPs should build a framework which can be used during Internal Business Reviews (IBRs) to determine the health of their big opportunity pipeline. As the founder of a CRM and Sales Enablement software company, I believe that high quality business reviews can only be accomplished with the support of tailored technology that offers transparency into big deals easily and efficiently. By providing structured guidance for large deals, salespeople and account teams will know the right thing to do, when, how, and with whom, during long and complex sales cycles.

The building blocks to a strong internal business review framework include:

1. The ability of the Sales VP to determine movement and momentum in the pipeline. They must be able to quickly distinguish between activity and progress, i.e., high activity doesn't always translate into progress. For large opportunities, movement should be based on milestones, not simply stage movement. Alerts should be triggered when momentum is lacking, which could jeopardize big deals.

2. The review should also yield an updated view of opportunities prioritized based on a scorecard, not simply revenue, or "gut feel". For example, the largest deals aren't always a top priority if they require significant resources and/or modifications of deliverables that would make these deals and accounts unprofitable. The review should also highlight flaws in the scoring process. In other words, if an opportunity scores high but shows unsuccessful, was there an error in the rating model?

3. Stakeholder mapping at a glance. Sales leaders should be able to spot flaws in the relationship map quickly. Examples of relationship map red flags include:
   a. Has the account team forgotten key stakeholders?
   b. Do we know their attitude and influence?
   c. If stakeholders are negative, what's the action plan to resolve?
   d. Has there been interactions or dialog, i.e, meetings or conversations?
   e. Do we lack clear next steps and relationship goals?

4. The framework should highlight competitive activity. The Sales VP should be able to determine the specific competitors for an opportunity but also spot trends. For example:

    a   At the deal level, who are the competitors and how do we plan to win?

    b   At a high level, are we seeing the same competitors over and over again?

    c   At a high level, what value is lacking if prospects stick with status quo?

    d   Do all account teams have access to the right competitive info & plays?

5   The framework should include an account focus on "Why?" It's extremely helpful if the CRM platform has a designated section under each big deal opportunity to address the matter of "Why." Alignment with the prospect is critical, and your sales platform should force this line of questioning. For example, information is captured and can be discussed during the business review about:

    a   Why should they care (to make a change)?

    b   Why this type of solution? What other options could they choose?

    c   Why now?

    d   Why us?

In my experience, the top Sales VP's do three things:

1   Hold regular and predictable internal business reviews.

2   Follow the above framework to ensure that the quality of the internal business reviews is consistently high.

3   Use a technology platform tailored for large deals as the tool to drive and support the framework.

PART FOUR

Sales Culture Plays

"I used to believe that culture was 'soft' and had little bearing on our bottom line. What I believe today is that our culture has everything to do with our bottom line, now and into the future."

–VERN DOSCH, AUTHOR, *WIRED DIFFERENTLY*

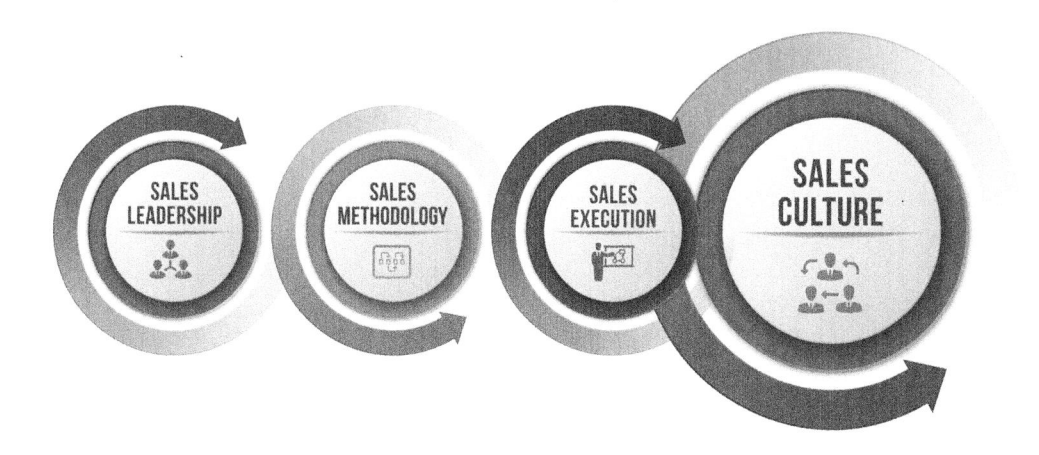

In this Part

5X Deal Sales Culture Involves

- Building a 5X deal sales culture
- Establishing executive outreach norms
- Celebrating 5X wins across your organization
- Debriefing, analyzing and defining repeatable best practices

Sales Leader Interview Findings

Top Line Sales, January 2019

I completed over 40 hours of live interviews with 41 Sales VP between February and October 2018. Among my findings was that a **Sales Leader Playbook needs to address Priorities and Best Practices**.

These are Top Sales Leader Priorities identified in our research:

- Revenue
- Recruiting and motivating sellers
- Team development
- Seller productivity
- Employee satisfaction
- Infrastructure to scale
- Pipeline growth
- Maximizing top accounts
- Market share
- Celebrating successes

Respondents indicated that a *sales leader playbook* allows leaders to rise above the urgent to focus on what's important.

The Top Sales Leader Challenges identified were:

- Recruiting and retaining the best salespeople
- Marketplace dynamics

- Training and skill development for sellers
- Commoditized product/marketing conditions
- Lack of data to manage the business
- Sellers' ability to follow the sales process
- Sales cycle is too long
- Friction among internal groups/departments
- Sales leader discipline to focus on what's most important
- Keeping up with the pace of change

Respondents indicated a *sales leader playbook* identifies best practices thereby driving consistency and accountability throughout the sales organization. Part Four: Sales Culture Plays deals with how to create and maintain that culture of consistency and accountability.

Take your team to the next level by creating your custom **Sales Leader Playbook**:

Downloadable templates make it easy for your sales leadership team to build your own unique approach to leadership, methodology, execution and culture for a 5X deal generating sales organization. No need to start from scratch. Customizable templates available at *www.toplinesales.com.*

PLAY #13

Build a 5X Deal Sales Culture

"Good is the enemy of great."

−JIM COLLINS

Play Attributes

Culture is broadly defined as that which shapes the everyday experiences of the team members. In terms of a 5X deal culture, it's usually crystal clear if a sales organization has a day-to-day focus on big deals or not. There are visible signs such as banners featuring logos associated with big customer wins, "ring the bell" announcements, war rooms with account strategy notes left on the white board and win celebrations. Note that there is a virtual equivalent for national or global sales organizations. It's also clear in the way that sales leaders and the executive team talk about landing big accounts. What stories do they tell? Are the stories about a team effort or an individual superstar? Strong *Big Deal* cultures have confidence in their system because they have a history of results, which creates an expectation of reliable wins in the future. The engine is in place and working, and that engine is driving the company's growth. A few more of the characteristics of a *Big Deal* sales culture include the following:

- Executive teams who are willing to invest in the right people with a desire and track record of winning big deals, training focused on development of large opportunities, programs, technology and other resources,
- Management teams that prioritize the long term vs. the short term when it comes to landing large accounts,
- Sales organizations that attract and retain top talent with a true enthusiasm for developing complex accounts,
- Sales leaders who set clear expectations, provide coaching and inspire account teams,
- Sales organizations that adhere to a proven methodology for identifying, developing, landing and growing truly large accounts with a methodology that is simply the way account teams work together to win,
- Account teams that have strong leadership, trust, and commitment to stay engaged and accountable over the long term,
- Organizations that encourage and align all resources, internal and external, to participate in strategic account development,
- Companies that have a solid structure to go after big contracts and maintain big customers,
- Account teams who celebrate big wins, and
- Sales organizations who do win/loss retrospectives and an authenticity around learning from the outcomes.

Constructing the Play

The best way to build a *Big Deal* sales culture is to take inventory of the current state followed by definitive plans for improvement. Decide on the most important components that make up the *Big Deal* culture for your company. For example,

- Do you attract and retain *Big Deal* talent?
- Does your sales structure lend itself to *Big Deal* development?
- Does your compensation structure reward 5X deals?
- Do you have clear expectations for execution of your methodology?
- Don't forget about war rooms, executive sponsor engagement and pre-call planning. We've included several models to assist with a comprehensive current state analysis. A true *Big Deal* sales culture will score fairly high in all areas.

Deploying the Play

1. Company leadership should do a 5X deal culture check-up looking for enthusiasm, motivation, trust, appropriate habits, effective communication, and desire to win.
2. Leaders should look for areas needing improvement within *Big Deal* results, processes, sales structure, people and culture.
3. Benchmark other divisions or similar companies, if possible, recognizing that small improvements make a big difference over time.
4. Make sure there are observable signs of a *Big Deal* culture.

Yellow and Red Flag Alerts

Examples of Yellow Flags

- Senior company leaders and stakeholders focus on 30-day business vs. long-term development of big opportunities.
- Programs are launched, such as a war room program, only to falter after a couple of months.
- Day to day priorities take over and the long focus on big deals is lost.

The sales culture or *how things are done around here* is a short-term focus on immediate transactions and firefighting rather than a long-term, proactive focus on truly big opportunities.

Examples of Red Flags

- Big deals are rare and tied to a unique set of circumstances rather than a proven system to identify, develop and close.
- Companies don't invest in systems, methodologies, resources, training or retaining top talent that are necessary to build and maintain a *Big Deal* culture.

Defensive Remedies

- Follow the best practices outlined in this Playbook.

- Sales leadership must take the lead in engaging senior company executives across all disciplines.
- Educate the senior company leadership team, including marketing, technology, human resources and others about the value of establishing a *Big Deal* sales culture. Engage them in your current-state assessment. Get their ideas for improvements. Ask for their commitment to participate with customers and prospects. Include them in war room sessions. Get their backing for investments and resources. If they participate in the vision, the culture will follow.
- Be patient; cultures are developed over time.

Playbacks

Check out the related Play #1 Inspire and Activate Account Teams.

Check out the related Play #3 Create a Blueprint for Cross-Functional Collaboration.

Check out the related Play #4 Mentor and Develop Account Teams.

Play Models

ORGANIZATIONAL ASSESSMENT: 5X DEALS

	Company or Organization view: Our company believes and lives by the following guiding principles...	Assessment: Green/Yellow/Red
1	Landing large (5x our normal contract size) accounts has a transformational impact on our company	XXX
2	Account strategy war rooms pay off with both new prospects and existing customers	XXX
3	Strong sales leadership, following a proven methodology, leads to winning big deals	XXX

Company or Organization view: Our company believes and lives by the following guiding principles...	Assessment: Green/Yellow/Red
1 Truly large contracts are complex and only gained through focus over time, patience and attention to strategy detail	XXX
2 Account teams must have a strong lead who has a strategic perspective and helps the team think long term while committing to short term tactical actions	XXX
3 Our organization supports and allocates the time and the necessary resources to win or retain TOP Line Accounts™	XXX

Company or Organization view: Our company believes and lives by the following guiding principles...	Assessment: Green/Yellow/Red
1 Our executive team makes themselves available for important account visits and programs	XXX
2 Our senior leaders and managers participate in account related strategy meetings and critical customer meetings	XXX
3 Our company values big wins and has win celebrations with the entire account team	XXX

Sideline Coach: Expert Opinion
Brian Burns, CEO at *b2brevenue.com*

In my experience, there are three foundational elements to building and sustaining a 5X deal culture.

1. Special sales compensation for big deals. The regular sales compensation plan should include a *Big Deal* section that includes the following:

    a. Sales comp that ramps up starting at your company's threshold for big deals.

    b. Timeframes that match the time it takes for your company to land a big contract. This might extend beyond your normal calendar year. Opening the comp window for big deals will keep sellers focused and motivated. They will be willing to make the time investments required if they know that the account will stay with them and that sales comp won't change.

    c If you require the sellers to identify their big opportunities that qualify for special compensation, allow them the flexibility to switch accounts if necessary.

    d Consider comp or a bonus for all account team members to promote cross-functional teamwork.

2. Company executives who are all in. The top executives set the tone, and if they have bought into a *Big Deal* culture, all others will follow. For example, top executives should encourage and welcome opportunities to host their executive counterparts. A good strategy is home office visits. Fly customer or prospect executives in for a day of exchanging ideas. Big decisions represent big risks for your prospects and spending time with their counterparts reduces that risk. Introduce them to the team--legal, CMO, COO, IT or others as appropriate. They may even want to understand your financial status. However, a day of bonding will open the channels of communication between your company and your prospect's company. Company executives who are all in are leading by example, which goes a long way to promote a *Big Deal* culture.

3. Company leaders understand that 5X deals aren't just bigger, they happen differently. The entire company must get behind the biggest opportunities, and behaviors must change. Everyone must rally around the need for more resources and maybe even unfunded investments. For example, if your company's standard onsite evaluation is 30 days, a truly *Big Deal* might require 120 days plus all your best resources. *Big Deal* cultures understand the need for creativity and out of the box thinking and ask 'how' instead of putting up roadblocks for the account team.

PLAY #14

Establish Executive Outreach Norms

"Opportunities are usually disguised as hard work, so most people don't recognize them."

–ANN LANDERS

Play Attributes

Executive outreach is critical to maintaining a *Big Deal* sales culture. Your company's senior leadership team must be engaged with key customers and prospects in a meaningful way. Existing executive relationships, exec-to-exec planning sessions, executive entertainment and executive sales calls are all positive examples of a strong executive outreach program.

Company executives should also make themselves available to the account team in addition to prioritizing customer and prospect interactions. They should attend key war room sessions and lend their input to the account strategy and goals. They will undoubtedly have ideas for developing insights based on the team's research. They can clear the path for exceptions or make resources available to win 5X deals. Lastly, they play an important role in providing recognition for account milestones and accomplishments.

Two core programs will extend executive reach and provide a framework for executive interactions: the executive-to-executive connection program and the executive briefing communication. Both can be used in conjunction with an annual high-level customer planning meeting.

Constructing the Play

Executive-to-Executive Connection Program

- Reserved for top customers and/or prospects.
- The goal is to formalize and maximize executive-to-executive relationships over the long term; therefore, the program should be a multi-year program.
- Sales leadership is responsible for establishing the program, selecting accounts, setting program expectations, keeping the calendar, issuing invites and facilitating the interactions and follow up.
- The program should include 2-4 executive-to-executive touch points per year.
- A balance of business touchpoints, such as a high-level planning meeting, and personal touchpoints, such as entertainment, is ideal.

The Executive Briefing Communication

The annual Executive Briefing Communication, reserved for top customers, can be a stand-alone executive summary type document or used in conjunction with an annual high-level planning meeting. An Executive Brief is a powerful, proactive way to engage executive sponsors by communicating the outcomes and impact associated with your products or services.

The goal of an annual meeting is to engage your company's executive and your customer's executive sponsor(s) in a planning/visioning session to create go-forward plans. Additionally, these sessions are a great time to recap key achievements over the past year by sharing your Executive Briefing Communication.

Benefits of annual executive communications sessions and a subsequent Executive Brief include articulating alignment between your company and their company and raising the level of awareness of past successes and future initiatives.

Documenting accomplishments becomes evidence of your successes and can be referenced later with your key executives or new contacts, paving the way for executive sponsorship and access into the future. These sessions also provide recognition, as appropriate, for day to day contacts and their good work while differentiating you and your company.

High Level Customer Planning Meeting

High level customer planning meetings are generally held with top customers annually, or whatever time frame makes sense for your business. Also referred to as a Customer Business Review, the meeting is designed to share goals, strategies, initiatives and expectations for the upcoming year. The planning meeting agenda should include a retrospective of the prior year, priorities for the upcoming year, opportunities for joint initiatives, the introduction of value-added resource people from your company, and agreement on touchpoints throughout the year and more as appropriate. Highlights and agreements from the meeting should be recapped in writing and shared with your customer and with the account team. It's nice to include a social component to the meeting as well, such as a meal or event.

Deploying the Play

1. Sales VPs should engage the executive team to get them on board with their participation in the 5X deal sales process.
2. Sales leaders should set clear expectations for the executive's role and time investments.
3. Sales leadership should build and manage the Executive-to-Executive program.
4. Quarterly validation of executive outreach can occur during internal business reviews.
5. Sales leadership and the account team quarterback should build and manage the Annual Executive Communications process and the Annual High-Level Customer Planning meeting.
6. Evaluate the program and make adjustments annually.

Yellow and Red Flag Alerts

Examples of Yellow Flags

- Not all companies' executives are willing to participate in the outreach process.
- Account team doesn't have a log or records associated with successes and impact over the past year.
- Sales leadership (or another designated department) hasn't developed an executive-to-executive program.
- Executive outreach programs were started but don't have a program owner or someone to manage and therefore have stalled.

Examples of red flags

- The account team doesn't have an internal executive sponsor or company leader willing to participate in the outreach process.
- The account team hasn't sold the value of executive-to-executive programs to their prospect or customer and there is no customer or prospect executive sponsor.

Defensive Remedies

- Follow the best practices outlined in this Playbook.
- Designate clear roles and responsibilities for all executive-to-executive programs.
- Show appreciation for all positive executive-to-executive engagements.

Playbacks

Check out the related Play #6 Commit to a Strategic Opportunity Development Approach: Advance Nine, Engaging Executives.

Check out the related Play #15 Celebrate 5X Deals across Your Organization.

Play Models

EXECUTIVE OUTREACH CHECKLIST

Account: _____   Date: _____

Executive: _____

Executive Outreach Items	Completed Yes/No
Account team engaged	
Conducted research and insights developed	
Executive's background: job history, professional associations, boards, publications understood	
Executive bio obtained	
Executive personality style identified	
Executive's priorities or areas of focus clear to account team	
Executive's areas of interest known	
Commonality or alignment areas between their company and your company detailed	
History with executive and your company uncovered	
Contacts in common researched	
Reasons why executive would find value in meeting discussed	
Executive Assistant contacted	
Win Themes™ designed	
Pre-call planning conducted	
Agenda developed	

CUSTOMER BUSINESS REVIEW SAMPLE AGENDA

Overview
Savvy AEs and AMs proactively set up CBRs on an annual, semi-annual or other regular basis. The agenda is carefully planned in collaboration with both parties.

Purpose
- Customer Business Reviews (CBRs) are a proactive, powerful interaction between your top customers or top channels and your company
- CBRs should include an executive-to-executive exchange
- Agenda for CBRs must be strategic, not tactical
- Consistency year over year leads to deep customer relationships and alignment between companies
- CBRs clearly demonstrate your strategic commitment to the account or channel

Sample Agenda Topics
- Introduction of new resources or team members
- Company updates (both companies)
- Executive exchange – vision or direction oriented
- Review of prior goal achievement
- Highlights of cost savings or process improvements
- Recognition of people for outstanding accomplishments
- Long term roadmap sharing (i.e., technology, programs, etc.)
- Relationship assessment
- Customer satisfaction/issue resolution/problem solving
- Mutual goal setting (new)
- Planning – short term and long term
- Wrap up and agreement on next steps
- Social aspect (i.e. dinner, outing)

> **Benefits of Customer Business Reviews to the Account Selling Team**
> - Access to executive sponsors, outside of a sales process
> - Visibility of your good work and results
> - Clarity and alignment of goals
> - Deep understanding of your customer's (or channel) direction and plans
> - Map for future projects which may include the need for your products and services
> - It's much easier to gain additional business from an existing customer than to find a new customer. Set the stage for expanded business
> - Clear next steps for projects and initiatives
> - Heads up on any threats
> - Expand your relationshp base and move existing relationships forward
> - Broaden the customer's view of your company

Sideline Coach: Expert Opinion
Steve Hall, Australia's leading C Level Sales Authority And Managing Director of Executive Sales Coaching Australia

Points of Executive Engagement: If you're the Sales VP and you want the executive team to engage in the sales process for truly big opportunities, they might have questions about the commitment. For example, how much time are you asking for and what do you expect them to do? Although the points of executive engagement may differ from organization to organization, here are a few thought starters.

- **Targeting:** The executive team will have valuable input into the targeting process for Whale opportunities. Whether you're developing top X lists (i.e. top 100) based on specific criteria or focusing on vertical markets, the executive team should lend their expertise. It's much more productive for sales and marketing to seek the input of the executive team early when it comes to targeting top opportunities. Additionally, once the target is established, executives will be expected to participate in programs such as peer to peer exchanges or seminars.

- **During the buyer's journey:** Peer to peer executive conversation will continue throughout the buyer's journey. Executives on both sides (your executives and your prospect's executives) are in a unique position to clear roadblocks and to allocate key resources.

- **Referral possibilities:** Executives tend to know other executives in the same field. Your CFO will know other CFOs and your CMO will know other CMOs. It's likely that astute account teams will ask your company's executives to tap into their network for referrals.
- **Beginning of the sales process:** Many organizations start the sales process for large opportunities with an attempt to gain their prospect's executive sponsorship for the project or simply to discuss priorities to determine if there's value for further exploration. Executives expect to meet with like executives, so a clever account team will use their company's executives for those meetings.
- **On-going cultivations of the relationship:** The account team needs to make sure that executive connections continue well after the contract is closed.

The 180° Flip: One of the best ways to engage your company's executives is to help them to think about the times when other sales organizations have tried (whether successful or not) to reach out to them. In other words,

- How did they feel about being contacted and qualified by junior sellers who don't understand their issues and who can't talk on their level?
- What did they appreciate about the outreach?
- Were there any aspects of the engagement process that they didn't like?
- What were their expectations for a quality outreach and subsequent meeting?

If executives expect their own sales teams to engage with their peers in other companies but aren't prepared to be part of the process, they must consider how willing they are to engage with other companies who have the same attitude.

This perspective will allow your executive team to be armed with a success model that will lead to their willingness to engage in the large opportunity sales process.

Set up your Executive for Success: There are three levels of qualification required to prepare your company's executive team for engagement.

1. The account team should cover all aspects of the normal sales qualification process to determine if the opportunity is real, that is, a reasonable fit.
2. Long term qualification. The account team should think strategically when it comes to engaging their executives with customer or prospect executives.

Is this the type of company that has problems we can solve in the long-term even if there's no immediate need? Many times, an executive dialog can open up possibilities that didn't exist prior.

3. Before the account team facilitates an executive-to-executive meeting, they need to do their due diligence to make sure that it will be a good fit for both executives. A showstopper on both sides would simply waste their time.

"Put Me in Coach:" Part of establishing executive outreach norms is setting the expectation with your executive team that they must be willing to take instructions from the account team. Executives might offer input into the account strategy or goals but once a meeting is set, they must be willing to yield to the collective voice of the account team. We can all think of disastrous examples of executives going Rambo or AWOL during a critical C-level meeting. For instance:

- Executives over-promising things that the team can't possibly deliver
- Executives talking about areas that don't make sense to the prospect executive
- Executives bringing up topics that the customer or prospect doesn't care about

Like top dignitaries, the executive has to be willing to follow the script developed during the pre-call planning process.

PLAY #15

Celebrate 5X Wins across your Organization

"Dream big! There are no limitations to how good you can become or how high you can rise except the limits you put on yourself."

–BRIAN TRACY

Constructing the Play

It's essential to celebrate all 5X sales successes. Securing a strategic outcome, whether a new customer project or contract, can take months or even years. Team members may come and go; but once victory is achieved, a celebration is in order. Not only does a celebration reward the account team for their commitment, planning and dedication, but also it reinforces the process and behaviors needed to land large opportunities. Celebrations go a long way towards creating a winning sales culture. Important points include:

- Internal selling team celebrations are a must for TOP Line Account™ wins.
- Win celebrations are important for team morale but also reinforce successful habits which leads to more wins.

- Win celebrations include all team members, not just the core team.
- Win celebrations can also include your new customer, as appropriate.

5X Win Celebrations are important…
- to recognize the selling team (Account team) for of a job well done,
- to create a win culture,
- to reinforce best practices, which can be replicated,
- to learn from mistakes,
- to ensure that account teams remember recognition during difficult sales times,
- to motivate high performance by means of appreciation,
- to gather success stories which can be shared with prospects, and
- to build further commitment by including your customer as appropriate.

Celebrate Milestones

Account teams should celebrate large milestones along the way, for example, gaining an executive sponsor, becoming a finalist after an RFP or blocking a competitor.

Deploying the Play

1. Get the word out in a timely manner.
2. Publish win wires or ring the bell announcements as soon as possible after a 5X win.
3. Conduct a win/loss retrospective customer interview.
4. Gather the team for a de-brief.
5. Brainstorm everything that went right in the sales process.
6. Note all the things that should be changed next time.
7. Compile any competitive intelligence gained.
8. Think about breakthrough moments or events.
9. Build your win story which can be told and retold by others.
10. Determine who else would benefit from learnings, i.e., marketing, partners.

11 Plan a celebration.
12 When determining who would benefit, take extra measures to ensure that no one is left out.
13 Focus on fun, recognition, reinforcement and motivation.
14 Invest in tangible gifts that will remind team members of the victory.
15 Sales leaders should provide formal and information recognition for account teams.
16 Account teams should be recognized for major milestones in addition to ultimate contract wins.
17 Engage internal company executives to provide account team recognition.
18 Consider holding a separate event with your new customer.

Yellow and Red Flag Alerts

Examples of Yellow Flags

- Account team milestones go unnoticed by sales leadership.
- Company executives aren't actively involved with recognition for account team accomplishments.

Examples of Red Flags

- Account team 5X wins aren't formally celebrated.
- Account team celebrations exclude account team members.

Defensive Remedies

- Follow the best practices outlined in this Playbook.
- Use the 5X Win Celebration Checklist.
- Block time on calendar each quarter for account team recognition.
- Work with account quarterback to provide day to day recognition of positive behaviors and accomplishments.

Playbacks

Check out the related Play #1 Inspire and Activate Account Teams.

Check out the related Play #9 Designate and Enable the Account Quarterback.

Check out the related Play #16 Debrief, Analyze and Define Repeatable Best Practices.

Play Models

WIN CELEBRATION CHECKLIST

5X Win Celebration Checklist

Have you considered/completed the following?
☐ Ring the bell or publish a *Ring the Bell* communication
☐ Gather the account team to help plan the celebration
☐ Consider everyone beyond the account team who was instrumental to the win and include them
☐ Make sure your celebration is fun, memorable and inspiring
☐ Invest in gifts that will be a tangible reminder of the victory
☐ Schedule a customer win retrospective
☐ Set a time with the account team to review learnings – customer perspective from the retrospective interview and the account team's perspective based on the selling process
☐ Compile all competitive intelligence gained and add to CRM
☐ Build the story about the win, which can be told throughout the organization
☐ Consider a separate celebration event with your new customer
☐ Debrief with your internal executive sponsor

Sideline Coach: Expert Opinion

John Golden, Chief Strategy & Marketing Officer, Pipelinersales Inc.

When it comes to celebrating really big wins, I would like to highlight a few best practices and several traps to avoid.

Best Practices

Successes should be viewed in a universal way. The organization must think about the Revenue Value Chain vs. the Sale. This adjustment is a culture-changing paradigm shift. When considering the revenue value chain for any large contract, the audience might include marketing, sales development, account managers and account executives, professional services, customer success team and customer service. Departments rarely operate in a vacuum; and with big deals, the lines are usually blurred.

Invest holistically. Everyone has access to basic tools like email and file sharing, but shouldn't everyone have access to the revenue pipeline (at least the dashboard)? Certainly, the CRM has replaced the old thermometer on the wall showing progress, but shouldn't the product development or the research and development team still be able to have visibility into the top level of big opportunities and their movement through the pipeline? Visual cues can create anticipation, excitement and intensification throughout the organization.

Acknowledge milestones as well as the ultimate contract win. Catch the account team and supporting cast in doing the right things. People come to work craving acknowledgement of a job well done.

Recognition becomes more challenging with global teams or virtual account teams. Gone are the days of installing a disco ball in the middle of the office and turning it on for everyone to see (and maybe even dance to) when something good happens. Yes, I actually did this! However, we need to mark our successes. We live in a world where the norm is to address a crisis or get to the bottom of what went wrong. It takes more effort and creativity but sales leaders can:

- hold video call celebrations
- place articles highlighting successes in internal enewsletters
- create engaging videos that include all members of the account team talking about the success

Sometimes, these modern techniques can lend themselves to greater focus, fun and attentiveness.

Traps

If you only recognize the end result, you miss all the leading indicators of success. For example, call planning and preparation are early indicators that account teams will eventually win.

Treating the forecast as a leading indicator. Trusting the forecast is a trap for sales leaders and salespeople. Salespeople feel most comfortable with a strong pipeline at the forecast stage and sales leaders trust that a forecasted deal is a done deal. A much stronger leading indicator is the depth and quality of the questions asked and answered during the qualify stage. The finest sales leaders will recognize account teams for taking whatever time is necessary to qualify big opportunities.

Account team resources who live by strict demarcations of what they do or their job description. Account team members must put their title and ego aside and put their oar in the water. The best account teams have members who are comfortable living outside the lines. Sales leaders should recognize and reinforce these attributes when they see them.

Sales celebrations that make others feel excluded. If only Sales is center stage for a big contract that was only won through the efforts of a large account team, morale will decline. It's better to error on the side of inclusiveness than leaving someone out.

PLAY #16

Debrief, Analyze and Define Repeatable Best Practices

"Our greatest weakness lies in giving up. The most certain way to succeed is to try just one more time."

–THOMAS EDISON

Play Attributes

The purpose of the win-loss retrospective process is to learn and grow as a *Big Deal* sales organization. The customer or prospect interviews uncover key learnings after a recent win or loss. The true voice of the customer offers a candid perspective and invaluable information, which are hard to gather through an on-line survey or during the sales process.

- Retrospectives yield new information including how and why the customer reached their recent decision.
- Learning about how the customer assesses value will lead to continuous improvements throughout the sales organization.
- The customer's point of view often reveals best practices which can be incorporated into future sales cycles.

Constructing the Play

- Prospect or customer interview should be conducted by someone familiar with sales process but not involved on a day-to-day basis. The goal is to create an environment where the customer feels comfortable offering candid feedback.
- Best if initiated within 30 – 90 days of win or loss.
- Prospects will view this process as positive and a differentiator for your company.
- Ask follow-up questions to the questions in the interview guide to uncover the more subtle aspects of the decision; for example, political pressure, risk associated with changing the status quo, social issues, etc. The goal is to find out what really happened.
- Avoid blaming when sharing learnings internally.
- Capture all learning and share internally to continue to improve institutionally.

Deploying the Play

1. Determine if the win or loss meets the criteria you established to conduct an interview.
2. Sales leader and account team determine best customer contact(s) for interview.
3. Sales leader initiates contact with customer and conducts meeting with customer.
4. Sales leader shares learnings with selling team and others in the organization who would benefit from learnings.
5. Sales leader documents interview results (call notes) of win/loss retrospective and posts to CRM or archives for future access.
6. Sales leader sends thank you note to customer.

Yellow and Red Flag Alerts

Examples of Yellow Flags

- Sales leaders don't set criteria for wins and losses which qualify for a retrospective interview.

- Sales leaders resort to blaming for losses.
- Sales leaders only conduct loss retrospectives, ignoring win retrospectives.

Examples of Red Flags

- Sales leaders don't conduct win or loss retrospectives.
- Retrospective learnings aren't shared with the account team.
- Learnings aren't institutionalized and thereby the organization doesn't benefit from the process.

Defensive Remedies

- Follow the best practices outlined in this Playbook.
- Account teams should meet before and after the win/loss retrospective. The before meeting should include pre-call planning, customizing interview questions and input from the team on key issues. The after meeting is to share, in a positive and constructive manner, the learnings from the customer/prospect interview.

Play Models

TOP LINE ACCOUNT™ PROGRAM WIN-LOSS RETROSPECTIVE INTERVIEW

Internal Background

Date: Interviewer: (Sales leader and/or designee)

Contact/Title:

Products/Services Proposed:

Customer Buying Scenario/Competitors:

Selling Team: (Including Partners)

Win ☐   Contract size: $

Loss ☐   If loss, who won?

Original source of lead:

Interview Questions

Can you provide general input (positives, areas of improvement) as it relates to the recent sales process?

What were your evaluation criteria/objectives? (Ask about business, financial, technical, operational criteria as appropriate.) Did your criteria change as you went through your buying process?

How did our company measure up to (or fall short of) your criteria? Ask for examples.

Can you provide an overview of what was most important to you with regards to our products and services?

Interview Questions

Can you provide an overview of your decision making process? (Try to uncover any factors such as political, social, risk factors that might have affected the decision. Ask about who was involved.) Were there dependencies that factored in throughout the decision making process?

Did our recommended product/services address the problem you were trying to solve? (Ask about impact and perceived value.)

What improvements can we make?

Please rate us versus the top company you considered in the following categories. (Use a 1-5 ranking: 1 = Strongest 5 = Weakest)

	Our Company	Leading Competitor
Responsiveness		
Understanding your needs		
Alignment with your objectives		
Sales approach		
Depth of team members and resources (incl. partners)		
Quality of proposal/presentation/demo		
Overall value		
Price		

Customer comments on any of the above areas: (Ask for examples)

In the case of a win: "Can you describe the biggest benefit to a business relationship with our company?"

In the case of a loss: "If given the opportunity, what would be the most important factor to gain your trust and earn your business in the future?"

Next Steps (for interviewer)

For a win, ask for customer references (letter or quote), white paper, case study, referral, as appropriate. Explore possible expansion opportunities.

For a win, recap the highlights and share with customer for reinforcement of their decision. If applicable, share with others such as internal champion and the executive sponsor.

For a loss, ask the customer if there are other areas of their business where your products or services might be of value. Also, ask for permission to follow up at an appropriate time in the future. (When?)

Ask them if you can add them to your newsletter, webinar or other nurturing lists?

Share findings with the selling team and others within your company. Was the strategy sound? Were your Win Themes ™ correct?

Send a thank-you note to the customer.

Update your CRM. Add them to any lists that they agreed to. For a loss, recycle to the Nurture Stage or Lead Stage of your sales process. For a win, recycle to the Expand Stage of your sales process.

Sideline Coach: Expert Opinion

Zeenath Kuraisha, Founder & CEO Asia Pacific Sales & Marketing Academy

In my role as CEO for the Asia Pacific Sales & Marketing Academy, I work with many large companies, some based out of the U.S., who have teams looking to land really big accounts. When it comes to organizational learning, I would like to highlight several big mistakes I've observed as well as more than a few best practices.

Big Companies Can Make Big Mistakes

To truly institute organizational learning, senior sales leaders need to be the driving force behind all big contracts. In APAC (East Asia, South Asia, Southeast Asia, Oceania) many of the account teams include both direct sales and a channel partner. I've observed significant instances of channel conflict as the channel partner may be partnering with competitors as well. Big mistakes can occur, especially when the stakes are high, if a senior leader isn't taking charge of the opportunity.

Another red flag that leads to account team conflict is when members of the direct/channel team are compensated differently. They may have vastly different financial motivations. One remedy to this issue is for senior company leaders to develop a common goal bonus or compensation structure. Minimizing artificial barriers such as financial rewards will lead to a culture of true teamwork around large account takedowns.

Best Practices to Promote a Culture of Big Deal Learning

Buy-in at all levels of the organization is critical. Learnings from the team on the ground must be shared with Marketing, Channel Partners, Business Development, Professional Services or anyone else who supports the end customer. The Customer Success Team is also in an excellent position to communicate customer needs, feedback and input to help the organization learn what works. One best practice I've observed is when senior company leaders participate in account team meetings. It's a big morale booster for the team.

Analyzing deals won and lost over a period of time can yield tremendous insights into the root causes, common issues and critical success factors. To augment this internal analysis, one of my clients sent their senior leadership team on a Listening

Tour to get firsthand input and feedback from their customers. These learnings were then shared throughout the organizations and changes were made where needed.

Another effective approach, especially in a tri-party (direct, channel, customer) situation, is a process to assess the total ecosystem of the large account selling process, for example, account plan audits that include deep, pointed questions designed to detect flaws in the account plan. The team can learn early what might go wrong and adjust in time to secure the contract.

APPENDIX 1

SIDELINE COACH: EXPERT OPINION CONTRIBUTORS

I would like to thank the generous contributions of the following experts. I searched the world for the right sideline coach for each play. Consequently, I ended up with intriguing and sound opinions from Europe, Australia, Singapore and all corners of the U.S.

Asia Pacific

Zeenath Kuraisha is a sales professional with more than 20 years of experience, providing inside sales advisory services from start-ups to enterprises. Her services range from creating sales playbooks to streamlining sales processes as well as helping companies ramp up their go-to-market efforts through sales enablement by creating and implementing global and regional demand generation strategies and sales programs. With a global reach, Zeena has worked on projects to increase both sales and customer experience with global brands like Microsoft, Oracle, Cisco, Google, Apple, NetApp and many other APAC and global inside sales organizations, communities and associations.

Australia

Steve Hall has been called Australia's leading Authority on Selling at "C" Level. Successful CEOs and sales directors of growing companies turn to Steve when sales becomes a bottleneck and they realize they need to sell more effectively at a higher level in their target accounts. As a devil's advocate and an Executive Sales Coach, Steve helps his clients eliminate the obstacles to higher sales.

Europe

Bob Apollo is the founder of Inflexion-Point Strategy Partners, the UK-based B2B value selling experts. He is a Fellow of the Association of Professional Sales, a member of the Sales Enablement Society, and a founding contributor to the *International Journal of Sales Transformation*. Following a successful corporate career spanning start-ups, scale-ups and market leaders, he now works as advisor, coach and trainer to a select client base of growth-orientated B2B sales organizations.

George Bronténn is the founder & CEO of Membrain, the Sales Enablement CRM that makes it easy to execute your sales strategy. George is a life-long entrepreneur with 20 years of experience in the software space and a passion for sales and marketing. With the life motto "Don't settle for mainstream," he is always looking for new ways to achieve improved business results using innovative software, skills and processes.

United States

Brian Burns is the host of two podcasts in the Top 15 in business on iTunes: *The B2B Revenue Leadership Show* and *The Brutal Truth about Sales and Selling Show*. He has authored four books on B2B sales and marketing drawing from his past 25 years of experience. Brian is the CEO of B2BRevenue.com.

Deb Calvert is the author of *DISCOVER Questions® Get You Connected* and the co-author of *Stop Selling & Start Leading*. She is the president of People First Productivity Solutions, founder of The Sales Experts Channel, and a UC-Berkeley sales instructor. Deb is an in-demand keynote speaker, sales and leadership trainer, and certified executive coach.

An experienced salesperson and marketer, **Lisa Dennis** is president and founder of ValueProposition.expert and Knowledgence® Associates. She is an international marketing and sales consultant, trainer, author and strategist. Her forte is in helping organizations develop and integrate customer-focused value propositions into the marketing and sales mix of B2B companies across a broad range of industries.

John Golden is the Amazon bestselling author of *Winning the Battle for Sales: Lessons on Closing Every Deal from the World's Greatest Military Victories* and *Social Upheaval: How to Win at Social Selling*. A globally acknowledged sales & marketing thought leader, speaker, and strategist, he is CSMO at Pipeliner CRM. In his spare time, John is an avid martial artist.

According to Forbes.com, **Alice Heiman** is among the world's leading experts on the complex sale. She is the founder of Alice Heiman, LLC, a leading sales consultancy for midsize companies, strategizing with sales leadership to grow sales. She's originally from the widely known Miller Heiman Group. Heiman co-founded TradeShow Makeover™ which is now a leader in preparing companies to close more deals from their investment in exhibiting at and sponsoring trade shows and events.

Krista S. Moore is the Founder and CEO of K.Coaching, Inc., a sales leadership coaching, consulting, and training organization. She is a sought-after motivational speaker, author, certified business coach, Retreat Leader and host of The Krista Moore Talk Show. Moore combines her real-life experiences leading sales for multimillion-dollar startups, Fortune 500 companies, and coaching successful sales leaders throughout the world.

James Muir is the CEO of Best Practice International and the bestselling author of the #1 book on closing sales, *The Perfect Close,* that shows sales professionals a clear and simple approach to close more opportunities and accelerate sales to the highest levels while remaining genuinely authentic. Those interested in learning a method of closing that is zero pressure, involves just two questions and is successful 95% of the time can reach him at PureMuir.com.

Suzanne Paling, a recognized leader in sales management, has over 25 years of experience in sales management consulting and coaching. She has helped more than sixty companies improve their sales performance and processes. Clients include product and service firms in the manufacturing, software, publishing, distribution, medical, and construction industries. Suzanne is the author of two award-winning books *The Accidental Sales Manager,* (Entrepreneur Press) and *The Sales Leader's Problem Solver* (Career Press).

Christopher Ryan, founder and CEO of Fusion Marketing Partners, is a business value and revenue growth specialist. He has 25 years of marketing, technology, and senior management experience, and is a widely known expert in business-to-business marketing, lead-to-revenue modeling, sales strategy, and business startups. Chris is a frequent speaker and author of six books on B2B marketing and business growth, including the recently published, *Expert's B2B Revenue Growth Playbook.*

Jay Tyler Consulting was founded several years ago to enable first line leaders to "accelerate revenue growth." This methodology was built around "Unlocking the True Potential" of each Sales leader. Jay's clients include Symantec, Veritas Corp, Rubrik, Tanium, vmware and many other Fortune 500 companies. Jay's former leadership roles include EVP of Sales and Marketing at Digital Think, Sr. VP of global sales at Clarify, an application software company, Group Vice President at Gartner, and National Sales Manager for Xerox Corporation.

Founder and CEO of The Whale Hunters®, **Barbara Weaver Smith, Ph.D.,** helps B2B companies grow fast by making bigger sales to bigger customers. For 20 years she has led growth-oriented companies to implement a complete business development system for selling successfully into large accounts, enterprise markets, including learning how to go global with global customers. Barbara wrote *Whale Hunting with Global Accounts* and *co-authored Whale Hunting: How to Land Big Sales and Transform Your Company.*

Daniel Zamudio is the founder and CEO of Playboox, a leading provider of Sales Enablement software and services. He is a thought leader on the convergence of process and technology to drive sales productivity and effectiveness and has consulted for global enterprises and fast-growth startups in the areas of sales leadership, sales process, sales messaging, and sales enablement.

APPENDIX 2

SALES LEADER INTERVIEWEES

I would like to express my deep gratitude for the following sales leaders. The research for this Playbook included comprehensive interviews with forty-one sales vice-presidents who graciously shared their biggest priorities and challenges and lent their perspective on what a Sales Leader Playbook should and should not be. Their wisdom informed the end result you now hold in your hand. I am profoundly grateful to each one of them.

- Gary Alton, EVP, Employer Services, The Partners Group, insurance industry
- Jim Andrews, Director of Sales, Viewpoint, construction software industry
- Jeff Antrican, formally Vice President, System Sales, United Technology Corporation, technology industry
- Aimee Arana, SVP & General Manager, Training Business Unit, Adidas, Germany, sports apparel industry
- Sacha Basho, Director of Global Partner Program, RiskSense, security industry
- Rupa Basu, formally SVP, Marketing, Corporate Accounts, Training and Strategy, BIOTRONIK, medical technology industry
- Jeni Billups, SVP, Marketing & Sales, OFD Foods, manufacturing industry
- Jay Blakey, Chief Development Officer, Salus Workers Comp, Inc., compensation insurance
- Lori Brown, formally Director of Global Sales Operations, Tektronix, technology industry

- David Brown, VP of Comcast Business, California Region, Comcast Business Services, business communications industry
- Shannon Burke, VP of Sales, Surescripts, healthcare industry
- Frank Capovilla, SVP, Global Sales, Ovum, technology research industry
- Jason Carr, VP of Sales, Central Region, AVI-SPL, technology digital workspace collaboration industry
- Mike Cembrola, VP of Sales, Delta Dental, healthcare industry
- Mike Dolloff, Chief Revenue Officer, Inflow Communications, professional services/technology industry
- Stan Earnshaw, VP of Sales, Next Stage Services
- Keith Forrester, VP, Marketing, Sales and Business Development, Kaiser Permanente, healthcare industry
- Brad Garrigues, Chief Sales & Marketing Officer, Providence Health Plan, insurance industry
- Jason Johnson, Executive Sales & Service, Providence Health & Services, healthcare industry
- Mark Ketchem, VP of Regional Sales, S&S Activewear, apparel industry
- Grant Lawson, Marketplace VP
- John Lee, Outsourced VP of Sales, Stumptown Sales Success, consulting services industry
- Regina Manfredi, VP, US Channel Sales, Crayon, software industry
- Terri Manley, Regional Business Development Director, NTT Data Services, global IT services industry
- Ed Manning, Director of Client Relations, Communication Concepts DFW
- Michael Maynes, Head of Sales, Cience, outsourced sales & marketing services industry
- Vince Meglio, SVP, Core Sales
- Lyndie Moore, SVP, Sales, SonoBello, medical/healthcare industry
- Ian O'Donnell, President, AI Analytics Services, Inc., software and consulting services industry
- Paul O'Mara, retired EVP, Sales, ID Experts, security industry
- Susan O'Sullivan, VP, US Sales, Ingram Micro, technology industry

- Jim Petrusich, VP, Global Sales, Northwest Analytics, software and analytics industry
- Jason Porter, VP of Sales & Marketing, Cayuse, research administration software industry
- Jim Robison, Director of Business Development – Risk, Security and Privacy, Online Business Systems, risk, security and privacy industry
- Steve Rybos, VP, Strategic Growth, GreatAmerica Financial Services, financial services industry
- Stuart Sides, SVP Strategic Accounts, BG Staffing, staffing industry
- Don Steele, CRO, Zeta Global, marketing services/technology industry
- Christine Stonesifer, VP, Western Region
- Cindy Thompson, Director, Healthcare Applications, Western Region, US Health & Lifesciences, Microsoft, software industry
- James Watson, VP of Sales & Operations, Best Pick Reports & Five Star Review, advertising/media industry
- Mark Wilcox, VP, North America Sales, Viewpoint, construction software industry

APPENDIX 3

CUSTOM TEMPLATES AVAILABLE AT WWW.TOPLINESALES.COM

Take your team to the next level by creating your custom **Sales Leader Playbook**. Downloadable templates make it easy for your sales leadership team to build your own unique approach to leadership, methodology, execution and culture for a 5X deal generating sales organization. No need to start from scratch – *The TOP Sales Leader Playbook: How to Win 5X Deals Repeatedly* includes definitions and samples for each template.

Sales Leadership Play Templates

- Sales Leadership Assessment
- Program Kick off Communication
- Big Deal Sales Expectations
- Cross Functional Collaboration: Team & Resources Prompts
- Account Team Coaching Questions
- Account Team: Can We Win? Assessment
- Training Reinforcement Guide
- Twelve Months at a Glance Calendar

Sales Methodology Play Templates

- Sales Methodology Assessment

Advances

- Scoring opportunities
- Gathering insights
- Assigning team and resources
- Agreeing on team guidelines
- Mapping relationships
- Constructing a pre-strategy SWOT matrix
- Charting strategy
- Designing Win Themes™
- Engaging executives
- Finding expansion opportunities
- Tracking progress
- 5X deal sales process framework
- Competitive strategy checklist

Sales Execution Play Templates

- Sales Execution Assessment
- Pre-Call Planning Worksheet
- Customer Meeting Agenda
- Successful Meeting Checklist
- Pre-Call Planning Effectiveness Assessment
- Pre-War Room Checklist
- War Room Agenda
- Internal 5X Business Review (IBR) Agenda
- Organizational Assessment

Sales Culture Play Templates

- Sales Culture Assessment
- Executive Outreach Checklist
- Customer Business Review Agenda
- Win Celebration Checklist
- Win/Loss Customer Retrospective Interview Guide

Top Line Sales offers three level of access*

1. Individual templates
2. Full playbook template
3. Expert assistance working with your sales leadership team to build your custom Playbook

*Need help customizing your Playbook?

Not sure which templates are the best fit?

Contact Top Line Sales, we can help.

Custom Templates Available at
www.toplinesales.com

ABOUT THE AUTHOR

Lisa Magnuson has walked in the shoes of sales leaders. She was an award-winning sales manager and led the charge as a Sales VP for several sales organizations across a variety of geographies, including executive positions with Fortune 50 companies. She has over 35 years of sales and sales leadership experience working with large and small corporate clients, across a broad spectrum of industries including technology, software, security, healthcare, medical device, insurance and manufacturing.

Top Line Sales, the company Lisa founded in 2005, has a proven track record of helping companies overcome the barriers to winning TOP Line Accounts™. These clients boast of closed contracts totaling over $350 million in new revenue due to Lisa's "roll up your sleeves" approach to help her clients win.

For the past fifteen years, Lisa has worked with senior sales leaders and their teams to achieve phenomenal results, especially in the area of big account wins. Lisa also founded and facilitated the Sales Executive Mastermind Group for Sales VPs in the Pacific Northwest. Recently, she conducted live, one-on-one interviews with forty-one sales executives (CRO's, Sales VP's and Directors) as part of her research for this book. All of these experiences have contributed to a fundamental and deep understanding of the unique priorities and challenges that sales leaders face, especially when it comes to building an organization to reliably deliver 5X Deals year after year.

Lisa is a published author of more than 250 articles on sales topics ranging from pre-call planning to landing TOP Line Accounts™. Her innovative webinar series, *Winning 5X Deals*, is heard monthly through the BrightTalk Sales Experts Channel (and available on demand). She is the author of *The TOP Seller Advantage: Powerful Strategies to Build Long-Term Executive Relationships*.

Printed in Great Britain
by Amazon